the **Greek** Travelmate

compiled by
Lexus
with
Irene M Cavoura
and revised by
Dr Costas Panayotakis

LEXUS

This new edition published 2004 by Lexus Ltd
60 Brook Street, Glasgow G40 2AB
Maps drawn by András Bereznay
Typeset by Elfreda Crehan
Series editor: Peter Terrell

First published in 1982 by Richard Drew Publishing Ltd, ISBN 0-904002-75-6
Published in 1991 by W & R Chambers Ltd, ISBN 0-550-22001-1

British Library Cataloguing in Publication Data
A catalogue record for this book is available from the British Library.

ISBN 1-904737-05-6

Printed and bound in Great Britain by Scotprint

Your Travelmate

gives you one single easy-to-use A to Z list of words and phrases to help you communicate in Greek.

Built into this list are:

- travel tips (✈) with facts and figures which provide valuable information
- typical replies to some of the things you might want to say
- language notes giving you basic information about speaking the language
- a menu reader on pages 80-83

There are maps of Greece and the Greek islands on pages 151-154. There is a list of common Greek signs and notices on pages 155-157. Greek numbers are listed on pages 158-159.The Greek alphabet is given on page 160.

Speaking Greek

Your Travelmate also tells you how to pronounce Greek with the translations being given first in a romanized form of Greek. Just read these pronunciation guides as though they were English and you will communicate – although you might not sound exactly like a native speaker.

In a few cases where the Greek translation is in fact an English word then this translation is put in quotes.

Stress

Letters in blue show which part of a word to stress, or to give more weight to, when speaking Greek. Getting the stress right is particularly important.

Some special points about the pronunciation system used to represent Greek:

e	like the e in w**e**t
eh	at the end of a word, also like the e sound in w**e**t
g	like the g in **g**o
i	like the i in p**i**tta bread or Mar**i**a
KH	from the back of the throat, like the ch in the way Scots pronounce lo**ch**
o	like the o in h**o**t
s	like the s in **s**oft
th	like the th in **th**is, sometimes close to a d
TH	like the th in **th**ing

You'll notice that a semi-colon is the Greek question mark.

Men and women speaking

When you see an entry like:

I'm a stranger here imeh ksenos/kseni etho [είμαι ξένος/ ξένη εδώ]

the Greek given after the slash is the form to be used by female speakers. So a man would say:

I'm a stranger here imeh ksenos etho

and a woman would say:

I'm a stranger here imeh kseni etho

When two versions are given, as in:

driver o/i othigos [ο/η οδηγός]
expert enas/mia ithikos [ένας/μιά ειδικός]

the first (o, enas) is for men and the second (i, mia) for women.

Language backup

To find out more about Lexus and Lexus Translations or to comment on this book you can go on-line to www.lexusforlanguages.co.uk.

a, an enas/mia/ena [ένας/μιά/ένα]

> The corresponding words for 'the' are o/i/to [ο/η/το].

about: is he about? ineh etho yiro? [είναι εδώ γύρω;]
about 15 peripoo 15 [περίπου 15]
above apo pano [από πάνω]
abroad sto eksoteriko [στο εξωτερικό]
absolutely! oposthipoteh! [οπωσδήποτε!]
accelerator to gazi [το γκάζι]
accept thekHomeh [δέχομαι]
accident ena thistikHima [ένα δυστύχημα]
there's been an accident eyineh ena thistikHima [έγινε ένα δυστύχημα]
accurate akrivis [ακριβής]
across: across the street apenandi ston thromo [απέναντι στον δρόμο]
adaptor ena polaplo [ένα πολλαπλό]
address i thi-efTHinsi [η διεύθυνση]
adjust riTHmizo [ρυθμίζω]
admission i isothos [η είσοδος]
Adriatic i athriatiki [η Αδριατική]
advance: can we book in advance? boroomeh na klisoomeh THesis apo prin? [μπορούμε να κλείσουμε θέσεις από πριν;]
advert mia thiafimisi [μιά διαφήμιση]
Aegean to eyeo [το Αιγαίο]
afraid: I'm afraid so fovameh pos neh [φοβάμαι πως ναι]
I'm afraid not fovameh pos oKHi [φοβάμαι πως όχι]
after meta [μετά]
after you meta apo sas [μετά από σας]

afternoon to apoyevma [το απόγευμα]
this afternoon simera to apoyevma [σήμερα το απόγευμα]
aftershave i kolonia ksirismatos [η κολώνια ξυρίσματος]
again ksana [ξανά]
against enandion [εναντίον]
age i ilikia [η ηλικία]
under age anilikos [ανήλικος]
it takes ages kani poli ora [κάνει πολλή ώρα]
ago: a week ago *prin apo* mia evthomatha [πριν από μιά εβδομάδα]
it wasn't long ago then pa-i polis keros [δεν πάει πολύς καιρός]
how long ago was that? prin apo poso kero itan afto? [πριν από πόσο καιρό ήταν αυτό;]
agree: I agree simfono [συμφωνώ]
it doesn't agree with me then moo kani kalo [δεν μου κάνει καλό]
air o aeras [ο αέρας]
by air a-eroporikos [αεροπορικώς]
air-conditioning: with air-conditioning meh klimatismo [με κλιματισμό]
air hostess i a-erosinothos [η αεροσυνοδός]
airmail: by airmail a-eroporikos [αεροπορικώς]
airport to a-erothromio [το αεροδρόμιο]
does this go to the airport? piyeni sto a-erothromio? [πηγαίνει στο αεροδρόμιο;]
airport bus to leoforio a-erothromioo [το λεωφορείο αεροδρομίου]
aisle seat mia THesi thipla ston thiathromo [μιά θέση δίπλα στον διάδρομο]
alarm clock to ksipnitiri [το ξυπνητήρι]
alcohol to alko-ol [το αλκοόλ]
is it alcoholic? ineh alko-oliko? [είναι αλκοολικό;]
alive: is he still alive? ineh akoma zondanos?

[είναι ακόμα ζωντανός;]
all oli [όλοι]
(everything) ola [όλα]
all night oli nikHta [όλη νύχτα]
that's all afta ineh ola [αυτά είναι όλα]
thank you – not at all efkHaristo – parakalo [ευχαριστώ – παρακαλώ]
all right endaksi [εντάξει]
allergic: I'm allergic to... imeh aleryikos/aleryiki sto... [είμαι αλλεργικός/αλλεργική στο...]
allowed: is it allowed? epitrepeteh? [επιτρέπεται;]
that's not allowed afto then epitrepeteh [αυτό δεν επιτρέπεται]
allow me epitrepsteh moo [επιτρέψτε μου]
almost skHethon [σχεδόν]
alone monos [μόνος]
did you come here alone? ilTHateh etho monos/moni sas? [ήλθατε εδώ μόνος/μόνη σας;]
leave me alone *(said by man/woman)* aseh meh isikHo/isikHi [άσε με ήσυχο/ήσυχη]
already ithi [ήδη]
also episis [επίσης]
although an keh [αν και]
altogether ola mazi [όλα μαζί]
what does that make altogether? poso kanoon ola mazi? [πόσο κάνουν όλα μαζί;]
always panda [πάντα]
am[1] *(in the morning)* to pro-i [το πρωί]

> Confusingly, the Greek abbreviation for am is pm [π.μ.].

am[2] *go to* **be**
ambulance ena proton vo-iTHion [ένα πρώτων βοηθειών]
get an ambulance! kalesteh to proton vo-iTHion [καλέστε το πρώτων βοηθειών]

✈ To get an ambulance dial 166.

America i ameriki [η Αμερική]
American *(man)* o amerikanos [ο Αμερικανός]
(woman) i amerikanitha [η Αμερικανίδα]
(adjective) amerikanikos [Αμερικανικός]
among metaksi [μεταξύ]
amp: a 13 amp fuse mia asfalia thekapendeh amber [μιά ασφάλεια δεκαπέντε αμπέρ]
anchor i angira [η άγκυρα]
and keh [και]
angry THimomenos [θυμωμένος]
ankle o astragalos [ο αστράγαλος]
anniversary: it's our anniversary ineh i epetios mas [είναι η επέτειός μας]
annoy: he's annoying me meh enoKHli [με ενοχλεί]
it's very annoying ineh poli enoKHlitiko [είναι πολύ ενοχλητικό]
another: can we have another room? boroomeh na eKHoomeh ena alo thomatio? [μπορούμε να έχουμε ένα άλλο δωμάτιο;]
another beer, please ali mia bira, parakalo [άλλη μία μπύρα, παρακαλώ]
answer i apandisi [η απάντηση]
what was his answer? ti apandiseh? [τί απάντησε;]
there was no answer then apandiseh [δεν απάντησε]
antibiotics to andiviotiko [το αντιβιοτικό]
antique mia antika [μιά αντίκα]

✈ Do not attempt to take with you any items belonging to archaeological sites (for example, stones or fragments of pots); you may have great difficulty explaining to the authorities that you were not really intending to steal items that belong to the cultural heritage of Greece.

any: have you got any bananas/butter? eKHeteh bananes/vootiro? [έχετε μπανάνες/βούτυρο;]
I haven't got any then eKHo kaTHoloo [δεν έχω καθόλου]
anybody kanis [κανείς]
anything tipota [τίποτα]
have you got anything for...? eKHeteh tipota ya... [έχετε τίποτα για...;]
I don't want anything then THelo tipota [δεν θέλω τίποτα]
apology: please accept my apologies sas zito signomi [σας ζητώ συγγνώμη]
appendicitis i skoliko-ithitis [η σκωληκοειδίτις]
appetite i oreksi [η όρεξη]
I've lost my appetite eKHasa tin oreksi moo [έχασα την όρεξή μου]
apple ena milo [ένα μήλο]
apple pie mia milopita [μιά μηλόπιτα]
appointment: can I make an appointment? boro na kliso ena randevoo? [μπορώ να κλείσω ένα ραντεβού;]
apricot ena verikoko [ένα βερύκοκκο]
April aprilios [Απρίλιος]
aqualung i bookala oksigonoo [η μπουκάλα οξυγόνου]

✈ Use of an aqualung requires a permit from the police.

•**archaeology** i arKHeoloyia [η αρχαιολογία]
are *go to* **be**
area *(neighbourhood)* i perioKHi [η περιοχή]
area code o kothikos ariTHmos [ο κωδικός αριθμός]

✈ Always include the zero of the area code. You also need to dial the area code even if you are in the same town.

arm to KHeri [το χέρι]
around *go to* **about**
arrange: will you arrange it? THa to kanoniseteh? [θα το κανονίσετε;]
arrest *(verb)* silamvano [συλλαμβάνω]
arrival i afiksi [η άφιξη]
arrive fTHano [φθάνω]
we only arrived yesterday fTHasameh molis KHtes [φθάσαμε μόλις χτες]
art i teKHni [η τέχνη]
art gallery mia pinakoTHiki [μιά πινακοθήκη]
arthritis ta arTHritika [τα αρθριτικά]
artificial teKHnitos [τεχνητός]
artist o kaliteKHnis [ο καλλιτέχνης]
(woman) i kaliteKHnitha [η καλλιτέχνιδα]
as: as quickly as you can oso pio grigora boris [όσο πιο γρήγορα μπορείς]
as much as you can oso pio poli boris [όσο πιο πολύ μπορείς]
as you like opos THelis [όπως θέλεις]
ashore stin ksira [στην ξηρά]
ashtray ena tasaki [ένα τασάκι]
ask roto [ρωτώ]
could you ask him to...? boris na too zitisis na...? [μπορείς να του ζητήσεις να...;]
that's not what I asked for then ineh afto poo zitisa [δεν είναι αυτό που ζήτησα]
asleep: he's still asleep akomi kimateh [ακόμη κοιμάται]
asparagus to sparangi [το σπαράγγι]
aspirin mia aspirini [μιά ασπιρίνη]
assistant o/i vo-iTHos [ο/η βοηθός]
(in shop) o/i ipalilos too katastimatos

[ο/η υπάλληλος του καταστήματος]
asthma to asTHma [το άσθμα]
at: at the café sto kafenio [στο καφενείο]
at the train station ston staTHmo trenon [στον σταθμό τρένων]
at one o'clock stis mia i ora [στις μία η ώρα]
Athens aTHina [Αθήνα]
attitude o tropos [ο τρόπος]
attractive: I think you're very attractive *(to man/woman)* nomizo oti iseh poli elkistikos/elkistiki [νομίζω ότι είσαι πολύ ελκυστικός/ελκυστική]
aubergine mia melitzana [μιά μελιτζάνα]
August avgoostos [Αύγουστος]
aunt: my aunt i THia moo [η θεία μου]
Australia i afstralia [η Αυστραλία]
Australian *(adjective)* afstralezikos [Αυστραλέζικος]
Austria i afstria [η Αυστρία]
authorities i arKHes [οι αρχές]
automatic *(car)* ena aftomato aftokinito [ένα αυτόματο αυτοκίνητο]
autumn: in the autumn to fTHinoporo [το φθινόπωρο]
away: is it far away from here? ineh makria apo etho? [είναι μακριά από εδώ;]
go away! fiyeh apo etho! [φύγε από εδώ!]
awful tromeros [τρομερός]
axle o aksonas [ο άξονας]

B

baby to moro [το μωρό]
we'd like a baby-sitter THeloomeh mia 'baby-sitter' [θέλουμε μιά μπέιμπι-σίτερ]

✈ Baby-sitters can be hired by the hour through travel agencies and hotels.

back: I've got a bad back eKHo provlimata meh

tin *plati* moo [έχω προβλήματα με την πλάτη μου]
at the back sto piso meros [στο πίσω μέρος]
I'll be right back THa yiriso grigora [θα γυρίσω γρήγορα]
is he back? yiriseh? [γύρισε;]
can I have my money back? boro na eKHo ta lefta moo piso? [μπορώ να έχω τα λεφτά μου πίσω;]
I go back tomorrow THa epistrepso avrio [θα επιστρέψω αύριο]
bacon to 'bacon' [το μπέικον]
bacon and eggs avga meh 'bacon' [αυγά με μπέικον]
bad kakos [κακός]
it's not bad then ineh asKHima [δεν είναι άσχημα]
too bad! ti na kanoomeh? [τί να κάνουμε;]
bag i tsanda [η τσάντα]
(suitcase) i valitsa [η βαλίτσα]
baggage i aposkeves [οι αποσκευές]
baker's o foornaris [ο φούρναρης]
balcony to balkoni [το μπαλκόνι]
a room with a balcony ena thomatio meh balkoni [ένα δωμάτιο με μπαλκόνι]
bald falakros [φαλακρός]
ball *(football etc)* i bala [η μπάλλα]
(tennis, golf) to balaki [το μπαλλάκι]
ball-point (pen) ena bik [ένα μπικ]
banana mia banana [μιά μπανάνα]
band *(musical)* mia orKHistra [μιά ορχήστρα]
(pop) ena singrotima [ένα συγκρότημα]
bandage o epithesmos [ο επίδεσμος]
could you change the bandage? boriteh na alakseteh ton epithesmo? [μπορείτε να αλλάξετε τον επίδεσμο;]
bank *(for money)* i trapeza [η τράπεζα]

✈ Open Mon-Thurs 8.00-14.00 and Fri 8.00-13.30; you'll need your passport; money can also be changed at points of entry into Greece (24-hour service), at some Telecommunication Offices (**OTE**) and post offices, at some hotels and in tourist gift shops (but the rates there are not as good as the rates in banks).

> *YOU MAY HEAR*
> to thiavatirio sas parakalo *your passport please*

bar to bar [το μπαρ]
in the bar sto bar [στο μπαρ]

✈ Modern bars are more expensive than cafés but more likely to stock foreign beers.

> *YOU MAY HEAR*
> ti THeleteh na sas fero? *what can I get you?*

barber's o kooreas [ο κουρέας]
bargain: it's a real bargain ineh pragmatiki efkeria [είναι πραγματική ευκαιρία]

✈ Quite common to bargain in Greece. But not in tourist shops.

> **that's too much** ineh para pola [είναι πάρα πολλά]
> **I'll give you...** THa soo thoso... [θα σου δώσω...]
> **I'll take it** THa to paro [θα το πάρω]

barmaid i servitora [η σερβιτόρα]
barman o barman [ο μπάρμαν]
baseball cap ena kapelo too 'baseball' [ένα καπέλο του 'baseball']
basket to kalaTHi [το καλάθι]

bath to banio [το μπάνιο]
can I have a bath? boro na kano banio? [μπορώ να κάνω μπάνιο;]
could you give me a bath towel? moo thineteh mia petseta banioo? [μου δίνετε μιά πετσέτα μπάνιου;]
bathroom to lootro [το λουτρό]
we want a room with bathroom THeloomeh ena thomatio meh lootro [θέλουμε ένα δωμάτιο με λουτρό]
can I use your bathroom? boro na KHrisimopiiso to lootro sas? [μπορώ να χρησιμοποιήσω το λουτρό σας;]
battery i bataria [η μπαταρία]
be

> Here is the present tense of the Greek verb for 'to be'.
>
> **I am** imeh [είμαι]
> **you are** *(familiar)* iseh [είσαι]
> **you are** *(polite)* isteh [είστε]
> **he/she/it is** ineh [είναι]
> **we are** imasteh [είμαστε]
> **you are** isteh *(plural)* [είστε]
> **they are** ineh [είναι]

be good na iseh kalos/kali [να είσαι καλός/καλή]
beach i paralia [η παραλία]
on the beach stin paralia [στην παραλία]
beans ta fasolia [τα φασόλια]
beautiful oreos [ωραίος]
that was a beautiful meal afto itan oreo yevma [αυτό ήταν ωραίο γεύμα]
because epithi [επειδή]
because of the weather logo too keroo [λόγω του καιρού]
bed to krevati [το κρεβάτι]

a single bed ena mono krevati [ένα μονό κρεβάτι]
a double bed ena thiplo krevati [ένα διπλό κρεβάτι]
I'm off to bed pao na ksaploso [πάω να ξαπλώσω]
you haven't changed my bed then alaksateh to krevati moo [δεν αλλάξατε το κρεβάτι μου]

bed and breakfast thomatio meh pro-ino [δωμάτιο με πρωινό]

✈ No equivalent to the British B&B in big towns. But in villages you could try a pansion [ΠΑΝΣΙΟΝ].

bedroom to ipnothomatio [το υπνοδωμάτιο]

bee mia melisa [μιά μέλισσα]

beef to moskHari [το μοσχάρι]

beer mia bira [μιά μπύρα]
two beers, please thio bires, parakalo [δύο μπύρες, παρακαλώ]

before: before breakfast prin to pro-ino [πριν το πρωινό]
before we leave prin figoomeh [πριν φύγουμε]
I haven't been here before then ekHo ksanalTHi etho [δεν έχω ξανάλθει εδώ]

begin: when does it begin? poteh arkHizi? [πότε αρχίζει;]

beginner enas arkHarios [ένας αρχάριος]
(female) mia arkHaria [μιά αρχάρια]

behind piso [πίσω]
behind me piso moo [πίσω μου]

Belgium to velyio [το Βέλγιο]

believe: I don't believe you then seh pistevo [δεν σε πιστεύω]
I believe you seh pistevo [σε πιστεύω]

bell to koothooni [το κουδούνι]

belong: that belongs to me ekino ineh thiko

moo [εκείνο είναι δικό μου]
who does this belong to? pianoo ineh afto? [ποιανού είναι αυτό;]
below kato [κάτω]
below the knee kato apo to gonato [κάτω από το γόνατο]
belt i zoni [η ζώνη]
bend *(in road)* i strofi [η στροφή]
berries ta moora [τα μούρα]
berth *(on ship)* mia klini [μιά κλίνη]
beside thipla [δίπλα]
best o pio kalos [ο πιό καλός]
it's the best holiday I've ever had ineh i kaliteres thiakopes poo ikHa poteh [είναι οι καλύτερες διακοπές που είχα ποτέ]
better kalitera [καλύτερα]
haven't you got anything better? then ekHeteh tipota kalitero? [δεν έχετε τίποτα καλύτερο;]
are you feeling better? esTHanesteh kalitera? [αισθάνεστε καλύτερα;]
I'm feeling a lot better esTHanomeh poli kalitera [αισθάνομαι πολύ καλύτερα]
between metaksi [μεταξύ]
beyond pera [πέρα]
beyond the mountains pera apo ta voona [πέρα από τα βουνά]
bicycle ena pothilato [ένα ποδήλατο]
big megalos [μεγάλος]
a big one ena megalo [ένα μεγάλο]
that's too big ineh poli megalo [είναι πολύ μεγάλο]
it's not big enough then ineh arketa megalo [δεν είναι αρκετά μεγάλο]
have you got a bigger one? ekHeteh ena megalitero? [έχετε ένα μεγαλύτερο;]
bike ena mikHanaki [ένα μηχανάκι]
bikini to bikini [το μπικίνι]

bill o logariasmos [ο λογαριασμός]
could I have the bill, please? boro na eKHo ton logariasmo, parakalo? [μπορώ να έχω τον λογαριασμό, παρακαλώ;]
bird to pooli [το πουλί]
birthday ta yeneTHlia [τα γενέθλια]
happy birthday! KHronia pola [χρόνια πολλά]
it's my birthday ineh ta yeneTHlia moo [είναι τα γενέθλιά μου]
biscuit ena biskoto [ένα μπισκότο]
bit: just a little bit for me mono ligo ya mena [μόνο λίγο για μένα]
that's a bit too expensive afto ineh *kapos* akrivo [αυτό είναι κάπως ακριβό]
a big bit ena megalo komati [ένα μεγάλο κομμάτι]
bitter *(taste)* pikros [πικρός]
black mavros [μαύρος]
blackout: he's had a blackout lipoTHimiseh [λιποθύμησε]
blanket i kooverta [η κουβέρτα]
bleach *(for cleaning)* i KHlorini [η χλωρίνη]
bleed emorago [αιμορραγώ]
bless you! *(after sneeze)* yasoo [γειά σου]
blind *(cannot see)* tiflos [τυφλός]
blister i fooskala [η φουσκάλα]
blocked *(pipe)* fragmenos [φραγμένος]
(road) klistos [κλειστός]
blonde i ksanTHi [η ξανθή]
blood to ema [το αίμα]
his blood group is... i omatha too ematos too ineh... [η ομάδα του αίματός του είναι...]
I've got high blood pressure eKHo psili pi-esi [έχω ψηλή πίεση]
he needs a blood transfusion KHriazeteh metangisi ematos [χρειάζεται μετάγγιση αίματος]

bloody: that's bloody good! afto ineh pragmatika iperoKHo! [αυτό είναι πραγματικά υπέροχο!]
bloody hell! *(annoyed)* gamoto! [γαμώτο!] *(amazed)* po! po! [πω! πω!]
blouse i blooza [η μπλούζα]
blue bleh [μπλε]
board: full board pliris thiatrofi [πλήρης διατροφή]
half board imithiatrofi [ημιδιατροφή]
boarding pass i karta epivivasis [η κάρτα επιβίβασης]
boat to plio [το πλοίο]
(small) i varka [η βάρκα]
when's the next boat to...? poteh ineh to epomeno plio ya...? [πότε είναι το επόμενο πλοίο για...;]
body to soma [το σώμα]
(corpse) ena ptoma [ένα πτώμα]
boil: do we have to boil the water? KHriazeteh na vrasoomeh to nero? [χρειάζεται να βράσουμε το νερό;]
boiled egg ena vrasto avgo [ένα βραστό αυγό]
bolt o sirtis [ο σύρτης]
bone ena kokalo [ένα κόκκαλο]
bonnet *(of car)* to kapo [το καπό]
book to vivlio [το βιβλίο]
can I book a seat for...? boro na kliso mia THesi ya...? [μπορώ να κλείσω μιά θέση για...;]

YOU MAY THEN HEAR
ti ora? *for what time?*
ti onoma? *what name is it?*

✈ Except for in very expensive restaurants it's not customary to book tables in Greece.

booking office to praktorio [το πρακτορείο]
bookshop ena vivliopolio [ένα βιβλιοπωλείο]
boot i bota [η μπότα]

(of car) to port bagaz [το πορτ μπαγκάζ]
booze: I had too much booze last night ipia poli *pioto* KHtes to vrathi [ήπια πολύ πιοτό χτες το βράδυ]
border to sinoro [το σύνορο]
bored: I'm bored var-yemeh [βαριέμαι]
boring varetos [βαρετός]
born: I was born in... yeniTHika to... [γεννήθηκα το...]
go to **date**
borrow: can I borrow...? boro na thanisto...? [μπορώ να δανειστώ...;]
boss to afendiko [το αφεντικό]
(woman) i afendikina [η αφεντικίνα]
both keh i thio [και οι δύο]
I'll take both of them THa paro keh ta thio [θα πάρω και τα δύο]
bottle ena bookali [ένα μπουκάλι]
bottle-opener to aniktiri [το ανοικτήρι]
bottom *(of person)* o kolos [ο κώλος]
at the bottom of the hill stoos propothes too lofoo [στους πρόποδες του λόφου]
bouncer o palikaras [ο παλληκαράς]
bowl *(for soup etc)* ena bol [ένα μπωλ]
box ena kooti [ένα κουτί]
boy to agori [το αγόρι]
boyfriend o filos [ο φίλος]
bra to sooti-en [το σουτιέν]
bracelet to vraKHioli [το βραχιόλι]
brake to freno [το φρένο]
could you check the brakes? boriteh na elenkseteh ta frena? [μπορείτε να ελέγξετε τα φρένα;]
I had to brake suddenly eprepeh na frenaro apotoma [έπρεπε να φρενάρω απότομα]
he didn't brake then frenareh [δεν φρέναρε]
brandy ena koniak [ένα κονιάκ]

bread to psomi [το ψωμί]
could we have some bread and butter? boroomeh na eKHoomeh ligo psomi keh ligo vootiro? [μπορούμε να έχουμε λίγο ψωμί και λίγο βούτυρο;]
some more bread, please akomi ligo psomi, parakalo [ακόμη λίγο ψωμί, παρακαλώ]
break *(verb)* spazo [σπάζω]
I think I've broken my arm nomizo oti eKHo spasi to KHeri moo [νομίζω ότι έχω σπάσει το χέρι μου]
you've broken it to espases [το έσπασες]
break into: my room has been broken into paraviasan to thomatio moo [παραβίασαν το δωμάτιό μου]
my car has been broken into paraviasan to aftokinito moo [παραβίασαν το αυτοκίνητό μου]
breakable efTHrafstos [εύθραυστος]
breakdown: I've had a breakdown KHalaseh to aftokinito moo [χάλασε το αυτοκίνητό μου]
a nervous breakdown enas nevrikos klonismos [ένας νευρικός κλονισμός]

✈ If you rent a car you'll get a phone number for the local **ELPA** [ΕΛΠΑ] or breakdown service. If you have your own car with proof of AA/RAC membership you'll get free help from the Greek **ELPA**; for information ring 174; for roadside assistance: 104.

breakfast to proyevma [το πρόγευμα]

✈ Greeks don't go for elaborate breakfasts; you'll get a continental-style breakfast of bread, jam, yoghurt and coffee at most cafés.

breast to stiTHos [το στήθος]
breathe anapneo [αναπνέω]

I can't breathe then boro na anapnefso [δεν μπορώ να αναπνεύσω]
bridge i yefira [η γέφυρα]
briefcase o кнartofilakas [ο χαρτοφύλακας]
brighten up: do you think it'll brighten up later? nomizeteh oti тнa kaliterepsi o keros argotera? [νομίζετε ότι θα καλυτερέψει ο καιρός αργότερα;]
brilliant *(person)* tetraperatos [τετραπέρατος]
(idea, swimmer) lambros [λαμπρός]
brilliant! iperoкнa! [υπέροχα!]
bring ferno [φέρνω]
could you bring it to my hotel? boriteh na to fereteh sto ksenothoкнio moo? [μπορείτε να το φέρετε στο ξενοδοχείο μου;]
Britain i vretania [η Βρετανία]
British vretanikos [Βρετανικός]
I'm British imeh vretanos [είμαι Βρετανός]
(woman) imeh vretanitha [είμαι Βρετανίδα]
brochure ena filathio [ένα φυλλάδιο]
have you got any brochures about...? eкнeteh kaтнoloo filathia ya...? [έχετε καθόλου φυλλάδια για...;]
broken spasmenos [σπασμένος]
brooch mia karfitsa [μιά καρφίτσα]
brother: my brother o athelfos moo [ο αδελφός μου]
brown kastanos [καστανός]
(tanned) mavrismenos [μαυρισμένος]
browse: can I just browse around? boro na rikso mia matia triyiro? [μπορώ να ρίξω μιά ματιά τριγύρω;]
bruise mia melania [μιά μελανιά]
brunette i melaкнrini [η μελαχροινή]
brush mia voortsa [μιά βούρτσα]
(painter's) ena pinelo [ένα πινέλο]
bucket o koovas [ο κουβάς]

buffet o boofes [ο μπουφές]
building to ktirio [το κτίριο]
bulb mia lamba [μιά λάμπα]
the bulb's gone i lamba ka-ikeh [η λάμπα κάηκε]
bumbag mia banana [μιά μπανάνα]
bump: he's had a bump on the head KHtipiseh to kefali too [χτύπησε το κεφάλι του]
bumper o profilaktiras [ο προφυλακτήρας]
bunch of flowers ena booketo looloothia [ένα μπουκέτο λουλούδια]
bunk mia klini [μιά κλίνη]
bunk beds i kooketes [οι κουκέτες]
buoy i simathoora [η σημαδούρα]
bureau de change ena grafio sinalagmatos [ένα Γραφείο Συναλλάγματος]
burglar enas kleftis [ένας κλέφτης]
(woman) mia kleftra [μιά κλέφτρα]
burgle: our flat's been burgled thi-eriksan to thiamerisma mas [διέρρηξαν το διαμέρισμά μας]

they've taken all my money eklepsan ola moo ta lefta [έκλεψαν όλα μου τα λεφτά]

burn: this meat is burnt afto to kreas ineh kameno [αυτό το κρέας είναι καμμένο]
my arms are burnt ta KHeria moo ka-ikan [τα χέρια μου κάηκαν]
can you give me something for these burns? boriteh na moo thoseteh kati yafta ta engavmata? [μπορείτε να μου δώσετε κάτι γι'αυτά τα εγκαύματα;]
bus to leoforio [το λεωφορείο]
which bus is it for...? pio leoforio pi-yeni...? [ποιό λεωφορείο πηγαίνει...;]

could you tell me when we get there? boriteh na moo piteh poo THa katevo? [μπορείτε να μου πείτε πού θα κατεβώ;]

✈ In towns you buy your ticket in advance from newspaper or cigarette kiosks. You have to validate your ticket when you get on by inserting it into the machine on the bus. Having done this you can't reuse this ticket.

business: I'm here on business imeh etho ya thooli-es [είμαι εδώ για δουλειές]
none of your business! then soo pefti logos [δεν σου πέφτει λόγος]
bus station to praktorio leoforion [το πρακτορείο λεωφορείων]
bus stop i stasi leoforion [η στάση λεωφορείων]
bust to stiTHos [το στήθος]
busy *(telephone)* apasKHolimeno [απασχολημένο]
are you busy? iseh apasKHolimenos/apasKHolimeni? [είσαι απασχολημένος/απασχολημένη;]
it's very busy here eKHi poli kinisi etho [έχι πολύ κίνηση εδώ]
but ala [αλλά]
not...but... oKHi...ala... [όχι...αλλά...]
butcher's o KHasapis [ο χασάπης]
butter to vootiro [το βούτυρο]
button to koompi [το κουμπί]
buy: where can I buy...? poo boro nagoraso...? [πού μπορώ ν'αγοράσω...;]
by: I'm here by myself imeh monos/moni moo etho [είμαι μόνος/μόνη μου εδώ]
are you by yourself? iseh monos/moni soo? [είσαι μόνος/μόνη σου;]
can you do it by tomorrow? boriteh na to kaneteh *meKHri* avrio? [μπορείτε να το κάνετε μέχρι αύριο;]
by train/car/plane meh treno/aftokinito/aeroplano [με τρένο/αυτοκίνητο/αεροπλάνο]

I parked by the trees parkara *konda sta* thendra [πάρκαρα κοντά στα δέντρα]
a film by... mia tenia too... [μιά ταινία του...]
who's it made by? pios to kataskevaseh? [ποιός το κατασκεύασε;]

C

cabbage ena laKHano [ένα λάχανο]
cabin *(on ship)* i kabina [η καμπίνα]
cable *(electric)* to kalothio [το καλώδιο]
café to kafenio [το καφενείο]

✈ Cafés serve food and (alcoholic) drinks; in cities they are usually open 24 hours a day; no problem with children.

cake ena 'cake' [ένα κέικ]
calculator to kombiooteraki [το κομπιουτεράκι]
call: will you call the manager? fonazeteh ton thi-efTHindi? [φωνάζετε τον διευθυντή;]
what is this called? pos to leneh? [πώς το λένε;]
I'll call back later *(on phone)* THa seh paro piso argotera [θα σε πάρω πίσω αργότερα]
call box enas tilefonikos THalamos [ένας τηλεφωνικός θάλαμος]
calm iremos [ήρεμος]
calm down! iremiseh! [ηρέμησε!]
camcorder mia miKHani lipseos [μιά μηχανή λήψεως]
camera i fotografiki miKHani [η φωτογραφική μηχανή]

✈ Cameras in museums and archaeological sites are usually permitted provided no tripod is used. Don't take photographs of military bases and airports.

camp: is there somewhere we can camp?

iparкнi meros na kataskinosoomeh? [υπάρχει μέρος να κατασκηνώσουμε;]
can we camp here? boroomeh na kataskinosoomeh etho? [μπορούμε να κατασκηνώσουμε εδώ;]
we're on a camping holiday kanoomeh thiakopes seh kataskinosi [κάνουμε διακοπές σε κατασκήνωση]

campsite to kamping [το κάμπινγκ]

✈ Be warned, there is no free camping in Greece. **EOT** (Greek Tourist Organization) has well organized sites.

can[1]: a can of beer mia bira *kootaki* [μιά μπύρα κουτάκι]

can[2]: can I have...? boro na eкно...? [μπορώ να έχω...;]
can you show me...? boriteh na moo thikseteh...? [μπορείτε να μου δείξετε...;]
(familiar) boris na moo thiksis...? [μπορείς να μου δείξεις...;]
I can't... then boro na... [δεν μπορώ να...]
he/she can't... then bori na... [δεν μπορεί να...]
we can't... then boroomeh na... [δεν μπορούμε να...]

Canada o kanathas [ο Καναδάς]

cancel: I want to cancel my booking тнelo na *akiroso* tin kratisi moo [θέλω να ακυρώσω την κράτησή μου]
can we cancel dinner for tonight? boroomeh na akirosoomeh to thipno ya apopseh? [μπορούμε να ακυρώσουμε το δείπνο για απόψε;]

candle to keri [το κερί]

can-opener to aniktiri [το ανοικτήρι]

capsize anapothoyirizo [αναποδογυρίζω]

car to aftokinito [το αυτοκίνητο]
by car meh aftokinito [με αυτοκίνητο]

carafe mia karafa [μιά καράφα]
caravan to troKHospito [το τροχόσπιτο]
carburettor to karbirater [το καρμπιρατέρ]
cards ta KHartia [τα χαρτιά]
do you play cards? pezeteh KHartia? [παίζετε χαρτιά;]
care: goodbye, take care andio, keh na proseKHis [αντίο, και να προσέχεις]
careful: be careful proseKHeh [πρόσεχε]
car-ferry to feribot [το φέρρυμποτ]
car park to parkin [το πάρκινγκ]
carpet to KHali [το χαλί]
(wall to wall) i moketa [η μοκέτα]
carrier bag mia sakoola [μιά σακούλα]
carrot ena karoto [ένα καρότο]
carry koovalao [κουβαλάω]
carving i gliptiki [η γλυπτική]
case *(suitcase)* i valitsa [η βαλίτσα]
cash ta metrita [τα μετρητά]
I haven't any cash then eKHo kaTHoloo metrita [δεν έχω καθόλου μετρητά]
will you cash a cheque for me? boriteh na moo eksaryiroseteh mia epitayi? [μπορείτε να μου εξαργυρώσετε μιά επιταγή;]
cash desk to tamio [το ταμείο]
casino to kazino [το καζίνο]
cassette mia kaseta [μιά κασέτα]
cassette player ena kasetofono [ένα κασετόφωνο]
cat i gata [η γάτα]
catch: where do we catch the bus? apo poo THa *paroomeh* to leoforio? [από πού θα πάρουμε το λεωφορείο;]
he's caught a bug *koliseh* mia arostia [κόλλησε μιά αρρώστια]
cathedral o kaTHethrikos naos [ο καθεδρικός ναός]
catholic kaTHolikos [καθολικός]
cave i spilia [η σπηλιά]

CD to 'CD' [το 'CD']
CD-player ena stereofoniko ya 'CD' [ένα στερεοφωνικό για 'CD']
ceiling to tavani [το ταβάνι]
cellophane to selofan [το σελοφάν]
cent ena 'cent' [ένα σεντ]
centigrade kelsioo [Κελσίου]

✈ C/5 x 9 + 32 = F

centigrade	-5	0	10	15	21	30	36.9	40
Fahrenheit	23	32	50	59	70	86	98.4	104

centimetre ena ekatosto [ένα εκατοστό]

✈ 1 cm = 0.39 inches

central kendrikos [κεντρικός]
with central heating meh kendriki THermansi [με κεντρική θέρμανση]
centre to kendro [το κέντρο]
how do we get to the centre? pos THa pameh sto kendro tis polis? [πώς θα πάμε στο κέντρο της πόλης;]
certain *(sure)* veveos [βέβαιος]
are you certain? iseh veveos/veveh-i? [είσαι βέβαιος/βέβαιη;]
certificate to pistopi-itiko [το πιστοποιητικό]
chain i alisitha [η αλυσίδα]
chair i karekla [η καρέκλα]
chambermaid i kamari-era [η καμαριέρα]
champagne i sampania [η σαμπάνια]
change *(verb)* alazo [αλλάζω]
could you change this into euros? boriteh na alakseteh afta seh evro? [μπορείτε να αλλάξετε αυτά σε ευρώ;]
I haven't any change then eKHo psila [δεν έχω ψιλά]
do you have change for 100 euros? eKHeteh psila ya na moo KHalaseteh ekato evro? [έχετε

ψιλά για να μου χαλάσετε 100 ευρώ;]
I'd like to change my flight THa iTHela na alakso tin kratisi moo [θα ήθελα να αλλάξω την κράτησή μου]
channel: the Channel i manKHi [η Μάγχη]
charge: what will you charge? posa THa KHreoseteh? [πόσα θα χρεώσετε;]
who's in charge? pios ineh ipefTHinos? [ποιός είναι υπεύθυνος;]
chart *(map)* o KHartis [ο χάρτης]
cheap fTHinos [φθηνός]
have you got something cheaper? eKHeteh tipota fTHinotero? [έχετε τίποτα φθηνότερο;]
cheat: I've been cheated moo ti skasaneh [μου τη σκάσανε]
check: will you check? boriteh na elenkseteh? [μπορείτε να ελέγξετε;]
I've checked eKHo elenksi [έχω ελέγξει]
we checked in kanameh 'check-in' [κάναμε 'check-in']
we checked out kanameh 'check-out' [κάναμε 'check-out']
check-in desk to 'check-in' [το 'check-in']
check-in time ora ya 'check-in' [ώρα για 'check-in']
cheek *(of face)* to magoolo [το μάγουλο]
cheeky afTHathis [αυθάδης]
cheerio yasoo [γειά σου]
cheers *(toast)* stin iya soo [στην υγειά σου]
(thanks) efKHaristo [ευχαριστώ]
cheese to tiri [το τυρί]
cheeseburger to 'cheeseburger' [το 'cheeseburger']
chef o sef [ο σεφ]
chemist's to farmakio [το φαρμακείο]

✈ Greek chemists will be able to help with minor medical complaints.

cheque mia epitayi [μιά επιταγή]

will you take a cheque? perneteh epitayes? [παίρνετε επιταγές;]

✈ Paying by cheque is not standard practice in Greece; only very big hotels, that have their own bank, accept cheques.

cheque book to vivlio epitagon [το βιβλίο επιταγών]
cheque card i karta epitagon [η κάρτα επιταγών]
chest to stiTHos [το στήθος]

✈ chest measurements

UK:	34	36	38	40	42	44	46
Greece:	87	91	97	102	107	112	117

chewing gum mia mastiKHa [μιά μαστίχα]
chicken to kotopoolo [το κοτόπουλο]
chickenpox i anemovloya [η ανεμοβλογιά]
child to pethi [το παιδί]
child minder mia dada [μιά νταντά]
children ta pethia [τα παιδιά]
a children's portion mia pethiki meritha [μιά παιδική μερίδα]

✈ Only hotels giving full board or half board serve children's portions; restaurants don't.

chin to sagoni [το σαγόνι]
china i porselani [η πορσελάνη]
chips i patates tiganites [οι πατάτες τηγανητές]
(in casino) i markes [οι μάρκες]
chocolate i sokolata [η σοκολάτα]
a hot chocolate mia sokolata rofima [μιά σοκολάτα ρόφημα]
a box of chocolates ena kooti sokolates [ένα κουτί σοκολάτες]
chop: pork/lamb chop mia KHirini/arnisia brizola [μιά χοιρινή/αρνίσια μπριζόλα]
Christian name to onoma [το όνομα]

Christmas KHristooyena [Χριστούγεννα]
  on Christmas Eve tin paramoni ton KHristooyenon [την παραμονή των Χριστουγέννων]
  Happy Christmas kala KHristooyena [Καλά Χριστούγεννα]
church i eklisia [η εκκλησία]

> ✈ Men should not be bare-chested; women should not wear short skirts.

cider ena 'cider' [ένα 'cider']
cigar to pooro [το πούρο]
cigarette to tsigaro [το τσιγάρο]
cinema to sinema [το σινεμά]
circle o kiklos [ο κύκλος]
  (in cinema) i platia [η πλατεία]
city i poli [η πόλη]
city centre to kendro tis polis [το κέντρο της πόλης]
claim *(insurance)* mia etisi ya asfalistra [μιά αίτηση για ασφάλιστρα]
clarify ksekaTHarizo [ξεκαθαρίζω]
clean *(adjective)* kaTHaros [καθαρός]
  it's not clean then ineh kaTHara [δεν είναι καθαρά]
  my room hasn't been cleaned today then kaTHarisan to thomatio moo simera [δεν καθάρισαν το δωμάτιό μου σήμερα]
cleansing cream to galaktoma kaTHarismoo [το γαλάκτωμα καθαρισμού]
clear: I'm not clear about it then imeh veveos/veveh-i yafto [δεν είμαι βέβαιος/βέβαιη γι'αυτό]
clever eksipnos [έξυπνος]
climate to klima [το κλίμα]
cloakroom *(for clothes)* i gardaroba [η γκαρνταρόμπα]
clock to rolo-i [το ρολόι]

close[1] konda [κοντά]
is it close to...? ineh konda sto...? [είναι κοντά στο...;]
close[2]: when do you close? poteh klineteh? [πότε κλείνετε;]
closed klistos [κλειστός]
cloth to ifasma [το ύφασμα]
(rag) ena kooreli [ένα κουρέλι]
clothes ta rooKHa [τα ρούχα]
clothes peg to mandalaki [το μανταλάκι]
cloud to sinefo [το σύννεφο]
clubbing: we're going clubbing pameh 'clubbing' [πάμε 'clubbing']
clutch to ambrayaz [το αμπραϊάζ]
coach to poolman [το πούλμαν]
coach party i omatha too poolman [η ομάδα του πούλμαν]
coach trip ena taksithi meh poolman [ένα ταξίδι με πούλμαν]
coast i akti [η ακτή]
at the coast stin akti [στην ακτή]
coastguard o aktofilakas [ο ακτοφύλακας]
coat to palto [το παλτό]
cockroach i katsaritha [η κατσαρίδα]
coffee o kafes [ο καφές]
two coffees, please thio kafethes, parakalo [δύο καφέδες, παρακαλώ]

✈ Greek coffee is always black and strong with a lot of grounds at the bottom of the cup.

YOU MAY HEAR
ti kafeh? *what sort of coffee?*
eliniko kafeh? *Greek coffee?*
neskafeh? *instant coffee?*
galiko kafeh? *filter coffee?*

sketo *without sugar*
metrio *medium sweet*
gliko *very sweet*

YOU CAN ASK FOR
a white coffee ena kafeh meh gala [ένα καφέ με γάλα]
a black coffee ena kafeh sketo [ένα καφέ σκέτο]

coin to kerma [το κέρμα]
coke® mia koka-kola [μιά κόκα-κόλα]
cold to krio [το κρύο]
I'm cold kriono [κρυώνω]
I've got a cold eKHo kriosi [έχω κρυώσει]
collapse: he's collapsed lipoTHimiseh [λιποθύμησε]
collar to kolaro [το κολλάρο]

✈ collar sizes

UK:	14	14.5	15	15.5	16	16.5	17
Greece:	36	37	38	39	41	42	43

collect: I've come to collect... iITHa ya na paralavo... [ήλθα για να παραλάβω...]
colour to KHroma [το χρώμα]
have you any other colours? eKHeteh ala KHromata? [έχετε άλλα χρώματα;]
comb mia KHtena [μιά χτένα]
come erKHomeh [έρχομαι]
I come from London imeh apo to lonthino [είμαι από το Λονδίνο]
come with me ela mazi moo [έλα μαζί μου]
come here ela etho [έλα εδώ]
come on! *(let's go)* pameh [πάμε]
oh, come on! *(disbelief)* psemata! [ψέμματα!]
comfortable anapaftikos [αναπαυτικός]
company *(business)* i eteria [η εταιρία]
you're good company iseh kali parea [είσαι

καλή παρέα]
compartment *(in train)* to thiamerisma [το διαμέρισμα]
compass i piksitha [η πυξίδα]
compensation i apozimiosi [η αποζημίωση]
I want compensation apeto apozimiosi [απαιτώ αποζημίωση]
complain thiamartiromeh [διαμαρτύρομαι]
I want to complain about my room THelo na thiamartiriTHo ya to thomatio moo [θέλω να διαμαρτυρηθώ για το δωμάτιό μου]
completely endelos [εντελώς]
complicated: it's very complicated ineh poli periploko [είναι πολύ περίπλοκο]
compliment: my compliments to the chef ta sinKHaritiria moo ston sef [τα συγχαρητήριά μου στον σεφ]
compulsory: is it compulsory? ineh ipoKHreotiko? [είναι υποχρεωτικό;]
computer enas ipoloyistis [ένας υπολογιστής]
concert i sinavlia [η συναυλία]
concussion i thiasisi [η διάσειση]
condition *(term)* o oros [ο όρος]
(state) i katastasi [η κατάσταση]
it's not in very good condition then ineh seh poli kali katastasi [δεν είναι σε πολύ καλή κατάσταση]
condom ena profilaktiko [ένα προφυλακτικό]
conference to sinethrio [το συνέδριο]
confirm epiveveono [επιβεβαιώνω]
confuse: you're confusing me meh berthevis [με μπερδεύεις]
congratulations! sinKHaritiria! [συγχαρητήρια!]
conjunctivitis i epipefikititha [η επιπεφυκίτιδα]
conman enas apateonas [ένας απατεώνας]
connection *(travel)* i sinthesi [η σύνδεση]
connoisseur enas/mia ithimon [ένας/μιά ειδήμων]

conscious: he's conscious eKHi tis esTHisis too [έχει τις αισθήσεις του]
consciousness: he's lost consciousness eKHaseh tis esTHisis too [έχασε τις αισθήσεις του]
constipation i thiskiliotita [η δυσκοιλιότητα]
consul o/i proksenos [ο/η Πρόξενος]
consulate to proksenio [το Προξενείο]
contact: how can I contact...? pos boro na elTHO seh epafi meh...? [πώς μπορώ να έλθω σε επαφή με...;]
contact lenses i faki epafis [οι φακοί επαφής]
convenient volikos [βολικός]
cook: it's not properly cooked then ineh kala psimeno [δεν είναι καλά ψημένο]
you're a good cook mayirevis orea [μαγειρεύεις ωραία]
cooker i koozina [η κουζίνα]
cool throseros [δροσερός]
(great) kool [κουλ]
Corfu i kerkira [η Κέρκυρα]
corkscrew to aniktiri [το ανοικτήρι]
corner i gonia [η γωνιά]
a corner table ena goniako trapezi [ένα γωνιακό τραπέζι]
on/in the corner sti gonia [στη γωνία]
cornflakes ta 'cornflakes' [τα κορν-φλέικς]
correct sostos [σωστός]
cosmetics ta kalindika [τα καλλυντικά]
cost: what does it cost? poso kani? [πόσο κάνει;]
cot to krevataki [το κρεβατάκι]
cotton to vamvaki [το βαμβάκι]
cotton wool to vamvaki [το βαμβάκι]
couchette i kooseta [η κουσέτα]
cough o viKHas [ο βήχας]
cough sweets i stagones ya ton viKHa [οι σταγόνες για τον βήχα]
could: could you...? boriteh na...? [μπορείτε

να...;]
could I have...? boro na eKHo...? [μπορώ να έχω...;]
we couldn't... then boroosameh na... [δεν μπορούσαμε να...]
country i KHora [η χώρα]
in the country(side) stin eksoKHi [στην εξοχή]
couple: a couple of... *(two)* thio... [δύο...]
(a few) meriki... [μερικοί...]
courier o/i taKHithromos [ο/η ταχυδρόμος]
course: of course veveos [βεβαίως]
court: I'll take you to court THa seh pao sto thikastirio [θα σε πάω στο δικαστήριο]
cousin: my cousin *(male)* o eksathelfos moo [ο εξάδελφός μου]
(female) i eksathelfi moo [η εξαδέλφη μου]
cover charge i engi-isi [η εγγύηση]
cow mia a-yelatha [μιά αγελάδα]
crab ena kavoori [ένα καβούρι]
craftshop ena magazi ithon la-ikis teKHnis [ένα μαγαζί ειδών λαϊκής τέχνης]
crap: this is crap afto ineh skata [αυτό είναι σκατά]
crash: there's been a crash eyineh ena trakarisma [έγινε ένα τρακάρισμα]
crash helmet ena kranos [ένα κράνος]
crazy trelos [τρελλός]
that's crazy afto ineh paralogo [αυτό είναι παράλογο]
cream i krema [η κρέμα]
credit card i pistotiki karta [η πιστωτική κάρτα]
Crete i kriti [η Κρήτη]
crisps ta tsips [τα τσιπς]
cross *(verb)* pernao apenandi [περνάω απέναντι]
crossroads i thiastavrosi [η διασταύρωση]
crowded yematos kosmo [γεμάτος κόσμο]
cruise i krooazi-era [η κρουαζιέρα]

crutch *(for invalid)* to thekaniki [το δεκανίκι]
cry: don't cry min kles [μην κλαις]
cup to flitzani [το φλυτζάνι]
a cup of coffee ena flitzani kafeh [ένα φλυτζάνι καφέ]
cupboard to doolapi [το ντουλάπι]
curry ena kari [ένα κάρι]
curtains i koortines [οι κουρτίνες]
cushion to maksilari [το μαξιλάρι]
Customs to telonio [το τελωνείο]

✈ It is illegal to take any stones etc out of the country that you may have picked up from an ancient site.

cut *(verb)* kovo [κόβω]
I've cut myself kopika [κόπηκα]
cycle: can we cycle there? boroomeh na pameh meh pothilato eki? [μπορούμε να πάμε με ποδήλατο εκεί;]
cyclist o/i pothilatis [ο/η ποδηλάτης]
Cyprus i kipros [η Κύπρος]

D

dad: my dad o babas moo [ο μπαμπάς μου]
damage: I'll pay for the damage THa pliroso ya ti *zimia* [θα πληρώσω για τη ζημιά]
damaged katestramenos [κατεστραμμένος]
damn! na pari i oryi! [να πάρει η οργή!]
damp igros [υγρός]
dance: would you like to dance? THelis na KHorepsoomeh? [θέλεις να χορέψουμε;]
dangerous epikinthinos [επικίνδυνος]
dark skotinos [σκοτεινός]
when does it get dark? poteh skotiniazi? [πότε σκοτεινιάζει;]
dark blue bleh skooros [μπλε σκούρος]

darling agapi moo [αγάπη μου]
date: what's the date? poses too minos eKHoomeh? [πόσες του μηνός έχουμε;]
can we make a date? *(romantic)* THelis na klisoomeh ena randevoo? [θέλεις να κλείσουμε ένα ραντεβού;]

> **on the fifth of May** stis pendeh ma-ioo [στις πέντε Μαΐου]
> **on the first of March** tin proti martioo [την πρώτη Μαρτίου]
> **in 1982** to KHilia eniakosia ogthonda thio [το χίλια εννιακόσια ογδόντα δύο]
> **in 2004** to thio KHiliathes tesera [το δύο χιλιάδες τέσσερα]

go to page 159
dates *(fruit)* i KHoormathes [οι χουρμάδες]
daughter: my daughter i kori moo [η κόρη μου]
day i imera [η ημέρα]
the day after tin epomeni imera [την επόμενη ημέρα]
the day before tin pro-igoomeni imera [την προηγούμενη ημέρα]
dazzle: his lights were dazzling me ta fota too meh tiflonan [τα φώτα του με τυφλώναν]
dead peTHamenos [πεθαμένος]
deaf koofos [κουφός]
deal: it's a deal simfoni [σύμφωνοι]
will you deal with it? THa to kanoniseteh? [θα το κανονίσετε;]
dear *(expensive)* akrivos [ακριβός]
Dear Costas agapiteh kosta [Αγαπητέ Κώστα]
Dear Maria agapiti maria [Αγαπητή Μαρία]
Dear Mr Papadopoulos agapiteh kirieh papathopooleh [Αγαπητέ κύριε Παπαδόπουλε]
December thekemvrios [Δεκέμβριος]

deck to katastroma [το κατάστρωμα]
deckchair i karekla too katastromatos [η καρέκλα του καταστρώματος]
declare: I have nothing to declare then eKHo tipota na thiloso [δεν έχω τίποτα να δηλώσω]
deep vaTHis [βαθύς]
delay: the flight was delayed i ptisi iKHeh kaTHisterisi [η πτήση είχε καθυστέρηση]
deliberately epitithes [επίτηδες]
delicate *(person)* leptos [λεπτός]
delicious yefstikotatos [γευστικότατος]
de luxe politelias [πολυτελείας]
dent ena vaTHooloma [ένα βαθούλωμα]
dentist o/i othondiatros [ο/η οδοντίατρος]

> *YOU MAY HEAR*
> pio thondi pona-i? *which tooth hurts?*
> anikseteh to stoma sas *open wide*
> ksevgalteh to stoma sas parakalo *please rinse out*

dentures i masela [η μασέλα]
deny: I deny it to arnoomeh [το αρνούμαι]
deodorant ena aposmitiko [ένα αποσμητικό]
departure i anaKHorisi [η αναχώρηση]
departure lounge i eTHoosa anaKHoriseos [η αίθουσα αναχωρήσεως]
depend: it depends eksartateh [εξαρτάται]
it depends on... eksartateh apo... [εξαρτάται από...]
deposit *(downpayment)* i prokatavoli [η προκαταβολή]
(security) i engi-isi [η εγγύηση]
do I have to leave a deposit? prepi na thoso engi-isi? [πρέπει να δώσω εγγύηση;]
depressed THlimenos [θλιμμένος]
depth to vaTHos [το βάθος]
desperate: I'm desperate for a drink peTHeno ya

ena poto [πεθαίνω για ένα ποτό]
dessert to epithorpio [το επιδόρπιο]
destination o pro-orismos [ο προορισμός]
detergent to aporipandiko [το απορυπαντικό]
detour enas parakamptirios thromos [ένας παρακαμπτήριος δρόμος]
develop: could you develop these? boriteh na tis emfaniseteh? [μπορείτε να τις εμφανίσετε;]
diabetic thiavitikos [διαβητικός]
diamond ena thiamandi [ένα διαμάντι]
diarrhoea i thiaria [η διάρροια]
have you got something for diarrhoea? eKHeteh kati ya ti thiaria? [έχετε κάτι για τη διάρροια;]
diary ena imeroloyio [ένα ημερολόγιο]
dictionary ena leksiko [ένα λεξικό]
didn't *go to* **not**
die peTHeno [πεθαίνω]
diesel i dizel [η ντίζελ]
diet i thi-eta [η δίαιτα]
I'm on a diet kano thi-eta [κάνω δίαιτα]
different: they are different ineh thiaforetiki [είναι διαφορετικοί]
can I have a different room? boro na eKHo ena *alo* thomatio? [μπορώ να έχω ένα άλλο δωμάτιο;]
difficult thiskolos [δύσκολος]
dinghy ena pliario [ένα πλοιάριο]
(rubber) mia lemvos [μιά λέμβος]
dining room i trapezaria [η τραπεζαρία]
dinner *(evening)* to thipno [το δείπνο]

✈ Dinner is normally available after 8 pm in tourist establishments. Greeks eat dinner between 9 and 11 pm.

dinner jacket ena smokin [ένα σμόκιν]
direct *(adjective)* efTHis [ευθύς]
does it go direct? pa-i katefTHian? [πάει κατ'

ευθείαν;]
dirty leromenos [λερωμένος]
disabled anapiros [ανάπηρος]
disappear eksafanizomeh [εξαφανίζομαι]
it's just disappeared molis tora eksafanistikeh [μόλις τώρα εξαφανίστηκε]
disappointing apogo-iteftikos [απογοητευτικός]
disco mia diskotek [μιά ντισκοτέκ]
discount mia ekptosi [μιά έκπτωση]
disgusting siKHamenos [σιχαμένος]
dish ena piato [ένα πιάτο]
dishonest atimos [άτιμος]
disinfectant to apolimandiko [το απολυμαντικό]
disposable camera mia fotografiki miKHani mias KHriseos [μιά φωτογραφική μηχανή μίας χρήσεως]
distance i apostasi [η απόσταση]
in the distance apo makria [από μακριά]
distress signal ena sima kinthinoo [ένα σήμα κινδύνου]
disturb: the noise is disturbing us o THorivos mas enoKHli [ο θόρυβος μας ενοχλεί]
diving board i sanitha ya vooti-es [η σανίδα για βουτιές]
divorced KHorismenos [χωρισμένος]
(woman) KHorismeni [χωρισμένη]
do kano [κάνω]
what are you doing tonight? ti THa kaneteh apopseh? [τί θα κάνετε απόψε;]
(familiar) ti THa kanis apopseh? [τί θα κάνεις απόψε;]
how do you do it? pos to kaneteh? [πώς το κάνετε;]
will you do it for me? boriteh na moo to kaneteh? [μπορείτε να μου το κάνετε;]
I've never done it before then to eKHo ksanakani [δεν το έχω ξανακάνει]
he did it aftos to ekaneh [αυτός το έκανε]

I was doing 60 kph etrekHa eksinda kHiliometra [έτρεχα εξήντα χιλιόμετρα]
how do you do? kHero poli [χαίρω πολύ]
doctor o/i yatros [ο/η γιατρός]
I need a doctor kHriazomeh enan yatro [χρειάζομαι έναν γιατρό]

✈ If you take the form E111 (obtainable from UK post offices) with you when you travel to Greece, this should enable you to get some free medical or dental treatment and pay for prescriptions at the local rate. Greek chemists will have a list of the nearest doctors' surgeries. Or take your E111 and passport to the nearest **IKA** office (Greek social insurance scheme) and they will give you the name of a doctor or dentist. You probably won't get a full refund though.

YOU MAY HEAR
to ekHeteh ksanapaTHi? *have you had this before?*
poo pona-i? *where does it hurt?*
perneteh kanena farmako? *are you taking any medication?*
parteh ena/thio apo afta *take one/two of these*
kaTHeh tris ores *every three hours*
thio fores tin imera *twice a day*

document to engrafo [το έγγραφο]
dog o skilos [ο σκύλος]
don't! mi! [μη!]; *go to* **not**
door i porta [η πόρτα]
dosage i thosi [η δόση]
double room ena thiplo thomatio [ένα διπλό δωμάτιο]
double whisky ena thiplo ooiski [ένα διπλό ουΐσκι]
down: down there eki kato [εκεί κάτω]

get down! kateva kato! [κατέβα κάτω!]
it's just down the road ineh ligo para kato [είναι λίγο πάρα κάτω]
downstairs kato [κάτω]
drain o oKHetos [ο οχετός]
(in bathroom) i apoKHetefsi [η αποχέτευση]
drawing pin mia pineza [μιά πινέζα]
dress to foostani [το φουστάνι]

✈ dress sizes

UK:	10	12	14	16	18	20
Greece:	36	38	40	42	44	46

dressing *(for cut)* mia gaza [μιά γάζα]
(for salad) to latholemono [το λαδολέμονο]
drink *(verb)* pino [πίνω]
(alcoholic) ena poto [ένα ποτό]
something to drink ena poto [ένα ποτό]
I don't drink then pino [δεν πίνω]
drinkable: is the water drinkable? to nero ineh posimo? [το νερό είναι πόσιμο;]
drive othigo [οδηγώ]
I've been driving all day othigoosa oli mera [οδηγούσα όλη μέρα]

✈ 100 kph (62 mph) is the maximum speed on motorways with 40 kph (25 mph) in town; seat belts are compulsory; be warned that Greek drivers are neither slow nor careful; *more at* **breakdowns.**

driver o/i othigos [ο/η οδηγός]
driving licence i athia othiyisis [η άδεια οδήγησης]
drown: he's drowning pniyeteh [πνίγεται]
drug ena farmako [ένα φάρμακο]
(narcotic etc) ena narkotiko [ένα ναρκωτικό]
drug dealer enas/mia emboros narkotikon [ένας/μιά έμπορος ναρκωτικών]
drunk *(adjective)* meTHismenos [μεθυσμένος]

dry *(adjective)* stegnos [στεγνός]
(wine) ksiros [ξηρός]
dry-cleaner's to stegnokaTHaristirio [το στεγνοκαθαριστήριο]
due: when is the bus due? poteh erkHeteh to leoforio? [πότε έρχεται το λεωφορείο;]
during kata ti thiarkia [κατά τη διάρκεια]
dust i skoni [η σκόνη]
duty-free shop ta aforoloyita ithi [τα Αφορολόγητα Είδη]
DVD ena 'DVD' [ένα 'DVD']

E

each: can we have one each? boroomeh na eKHoomeh ena o *kaTHenas*? [μπορούμε να έχουμε ένα ο καθένας;]
how much are they each? poso eKHi to kaTHena? [πόσο έχει το καθένα;]
ear to afti [το αυτί]
I've got earache pona-i to afti moo [πονάει το αυτί μου]
early noris [νωρίς]
we want to leave a day earlier THeloomeh na figoomeh mia mera noritera [θέλουμε να φύγουμε μία μέρα νωρίτερα]
earring to skoolariki [το σκουλαρίκι]
east i anatoli [η ανατολή]
Easter to paskHa [το Πάσχα]

✈ By far the most important festival and taken much more seriously than in the rest of western Europe. People may say 'kHristos anesti' *Christ is Risen* as a form of greeting.

YOU MAY HEAR
kalo paskHa *happy Easter*

Easter Monday i theftera too paskHa [η Δευτέρα του Πάσχα]
easy efkolos [εύκολος]
eat trogo [τρώγω]
something to eat kati na fao [κάτι να φάω]
egg ena avgo [ένα αυγό]
either: either... or... i...i... [ή...ή...]
I don't like either then moo aresi ooteh to ena ooteh to alo [δεν μου αρέσει ούτε το ένα ούτε το άλλο]
elastic elastikos [ελαστικός]
elastic band mia elastiki tenia [μιά ελαστική ταινία]
elbow o angonas [ο αγκώνας]
electric ilektrikos [ηλεκτρικός]
electric fire mia ilektriki somba [μιά ηλεκτρική σόμπα]
electrician o ilektrologos [ο ηλεκτρολόγος]
electricity o ilektrismos [ο ηλεκτρισμός]

✈ Voltage is 220, as in the UK. Most Greek plugs have two round pins, so a travel plug is essential for your own stuff.

elegant kompsos [κομψός]
else: something else kati alo [κάτι άλλο]
somewhere else kapoo aloo [κάπου αλλού]
who else? pios alos? [ποιός άλλος;]
or else ithalos [ειδάλλως]
email ena ilektroniko minima [ένα ηλεκτρονικό μήνυμα]
email me stileh moo ena ilektroniko minima [στείλε μου ένα ηλεκτρονικό μήνυμα]
email address i ilektroniki thi-efTHinsi [η ηλεκτρονική διεύθυνση]
what's your email address? pia ineh i ilektroniki thi-efTHinsi soo? [ποιά είναι η ηλεκτρονική διεύθυνσή σου;]

YOU MAY THEN HEAR
i ilektroniki thi-efTHinsi moo ineh...
papaki... telia...
my email address is...
at... dot...

embarrassed: I'm embarrassed vriskomeh seh amiKHania [βρίσκομαι σε αμηχανία]
embarrassing ferni seh amiKHania [φέρνει σε αμηχανία]
embassy i presvia [η Πρεσβεία]
emergency mia epigoosa anangi [μιά επείγουσα ανάγκη]
empty athios [άδειος]
end to telos [το τέλος]
when does it end? poteh telioni? [πότε τελειώνει;]
engaged *(telephone)* apasKHolimeno [απασχολημένο]
(toilet) katilimeni [κατειλημμένη]
(person) aravoniasmenos [αρραβωνιασμένος]
engagement ring i vera [η βέρα]
engine i miKHani [η μηχανή]
engine trouble provlima meh ti miKHani [πρόβλημα με τη μηχανή]
England i anglia [η Αγγλία]
English anglikos [Αγγλικός]
(language) ta anglika [τα Αγγλικά]
the English i angli [οι 'Αγγλοι]
Englishman o englezos [ο Εγγλέζος]
Englishwoman i engleza [η Εγγλέζα]
enjoy: I enjoyed it very much moo areseh para poli [μου άρεσε πάρα πολύ]
enjoy yourself kali thiaskethasi [καλή διασκέδαση]
enlargement *(photo)* mia meyeTHinsi [μιά μεγέθυνση]

enormous terastios [τεράστιος]
enough arketos [αρκετός]
that's not big enough afto then ineh arketa megalo [αυτό δεν είναι αρκετά μεγάλο]
I don't have enough money then eKHo arketa KHrimata [δεν έχω αρκετά χρήματα]
thank you, that's enough efKHaristo, ftani [ευχαριστώ, φτάνει]
ensuite: is it ensuite? eKHi banio to ipnothomatio? [έχει μπάνιο το υπνοδωμάτιο;]
entertainment i thiaskethasi [η διασκέδαση]
entrance i isothos [η είσοδος]
envelope o fakelos [ο φάκελλος]
error ena laTHos [ένα λάθος]
escalator i kiliomeni skala [η κυλιώμενη σκάλα]
especially kirios [κυρίως]
essential vasikos [βασικός]
e-ticket ena ilektroniko isitirio [ένα ηλεκτρονικό εισιτήριο]
euro ena evro [ένα ευρώ]
Europe i evropi [η Ευρώπη]
even: even the British *akomi keh* i vretani [ακόμη και οι Βρεταννοί]
evening to vrathi [το βράδυ]
this evening simera to vrathi [σήμερα το βράδυ]
good evening kalispera [καλησπέρα]
evening dress *(for man)* episimo enthima [επίσημο ένδυμα]
(for woman) vrathino forema [βραδυνό φόρεμα]
ever: have you ever been to...? eKHeteh pa-i poteh sto...? [έχετε πάει ποτέ στο...;]
every kaTHeh [κάθε]
everyone kaTHenas [καθένας]
is everyone ready? ineh oli etimi? [είναι όλοι έτοιμοι;]
everything ola [όλα]

everywhere pandoo [παντού]
exact akrivis [ακριβής]
example to parathigma [το παράδειγμα]
for example parathigmatos KHari [παραδείγματος χάρη]
excellent eksoKHos [έξοχος]
except: except me ektos apo mena [εκτός από μένα]
excess baggage to ipervaro [το υπέρβαρο]
exchange rate i sinalagmatiki isotimia [η συναλλαγματική ισοτιμία]
excursion mia ekthromi [μιά εκδρομή]
excuse me *(to get past etc)* meh sinKHoriteh [με συγχωρείτε]
(to get attention) sas parakalo [σας παρακαλώ]
(apology) zito signomi [ζητώ συγγνώμη]
exhaust *(on car)* i eksatmisi [η εξάτμιση]
exhausted eksandlimenos [εξαντλημένος]
exhibition i ekTHesi [η έκθεση]
exit i eksothos [η έξοδος]
expect: she's expecting perimeni pethi [περιμένει παιδί]
expensive akrivos [ακριβός]
that's too expensive afto ineh poli akrivo [αυτό είναι πολύ ακριβό]
expert enas/mia ithikos [ένας/μιά ειδικός]
explain eksigo [εξηγώ]
would you explain that slowly? boriteh na to eksiyiseteh afto arga? [μπορείτε να το εξηγήσετε αυτό αργά;]
extension cable mia pro-ektasi [μιά προέκταση]
extra: an extra day mia mera ekstra [μιά μέρα έξτρα]
is that extra? ekino ineh ekstra? [εκείνο είναι έξτρα;]
extremely ipervolika [υπερβολικά]
eye to mati [το μάτι]

eyebrow to frithi [το φρύδι]
eyebrow pencil ena molivi ya ta frithia [ένα μολύβι για τα φρύδια]
eyeliner ena 'eyeliner' [ένα 'eyeliner']
eye shadow i skia ya ta matia [η σκιά για τα μάτια]
eye witness enas/mia aftoptis martiras [ένας/μιά αυτόπτης μάρτυρας]

F

face to prosopo [το πρόσωπο]
face mask *(for diving)* i maska [η μάσκα]
fact to yegonos [το γεγονός]
factory to ergostasio [το εργοστάσιο]
Fahrenheit farenait [Φαρενάιτ]

✈ F – 32 x 5/9 = C

Fahrenheit	32	50	59	70	86	98.4	104
centigrade	0	10	15	21	30	36.9	40

faint: she's fainted lipoTHimiseh [λιποθύμησε]
fair *(fun-)* to paniyiri [το πανηγύρι]
(commercial) i ekTHesi [η έκθεση]
that's not fair then ineh thikeo [δεν είναι δίκαιο]
fake mia apati [μιά απάτη]
fall: he's fallen epeseh [έπεσε]
false pseftikos [ψεύτικος]
false teeth i masela [η μασέλα]
family i ikoyenia [η οικογένεια]
fan *(cooling)* o anemistiras [ο ανεμιστήρας]
(hand-held) i ventalia [η βεντάλια]
(supporter) o opathos [ο οπαδός]
fan belt to loori too ventilater [το λουρί του βεντιλατέρ]
far makria [μακριά]
is it far? ineh makria? [είναι μακριά;]

how far is it? poso makria ineh? [πόσο μακριά είναι;]
fare *(travel)* ta navla [τα ναύλα]
farm i farma [η φάρμα]
farther pio makria [πιό μακριά]
fashion i motha [η μόδα]
fast *(adjective)* grigoros [γρήγορος]
don't speak so fast mi milas toso grigora [μη μιλάς τόσο γρήγορα]
fat *(adjective)* KHondros [χοντρός]
father: my father o pateras moo [ο πατέρας μου]
fathom mia orya [μιά οργυιά]
fault *(defect)* mia vlavi [μιά βλάβη]
it's not my fault then fteo ego [δεν φταίω εγώ]
faulty elatomatikos [ελαττωματικός]
favourite *(adjective)* agapimenos [αγαπημένος]
fax ena 'fax' [ένα 'fax']
can you fax this for me? boriteh na to stileteh afto meh 'fax'? [μπορείτε να το στείλετε αυτό με 'fax';]
February fevrooarios [Φεβρουάριος]
fed-up: I'm fed-up booKHtisa [μπούχτισα]
feel: I feel like a... *(I want)* THa iTHela ena... [θα ήθελα ένα...]
felt-tip enas markathoros [ένας μαρκαδόρος]
ferry to feribot [το φέρρυμποτ]
fetch: will you come and fetch me? THa elTHis na meh paris? [θά έλθεις να με πάρεις;]
fever o piretos [ο πυρετός]
few: only a few mono liyi [μόνο λίγοι]
a few days liyes meres [λίγες μέρες]
fiancé o aravoniastikos [ο αρραβωνιαστικός]
fiancée i aravoniastikia [η αρραβωνιαστικιά]
fiddle: it's a fiddle ineh kobina [είναι κομπίνα]
field to KHorafi [το χωράφι]
(grass) to grasithi [το γρασίδι]
fifty-fifty misa-misa [μισά-μισά]

figs ta sika [τα σύκα]
figure *(number)* o ariTHmos [ο αριθμός]
(of person) i silooeta [η σιλουέτα]
fill: fill her up yemiseh to [γέμισέ το]
to fill in a form simplirono ena endipo [συμπληρώνω ένα έντυπο]
fillet to fileto [το φιλέτο]
filling *(in tooth)* to sfrayisma [το σφράγισμα]
film *(for camera)* to film [το φιλμ]
(at cinema) i tenia [η ταινία]
filter to filtro [το φίλτρο]
find vrisko [βρίσκω]
if you find it an to vris [αν το βρεις]
I've found a… vrika ena… [βρήκα ένα…]
fine *(weather)* oreos [ωραίος]
ok, that's fine endaksi, orea [εντάξει, ωραία]
a 100 euro fine ena prostimo 100 evro [ένα πρόστιμο 100 ευρώ]
finger to thaktilo [το δάκτυλο]
fingernail to niKHi [το νύχι]
finish: I haven't finished then teliosa [δεν τελείωσα]
when does it finish? poteh telioni? [πότε τελειώνει;]
fire mia fotia [μιά φωτιά]
(blaze: house on fire etc) mia pirkaya [μιά πυρκαϊά]
fire! fotia! [φωτιά!]
can we light a fire here? boroomeh na anapsoomeh fotia etho? [μπορούμε να ανάψουμε φωτιά εδώ;]
it's not firing *(car)* then ksekina-i [δεν ξεκινάει]
fire brigade i pirosvestiki [η πυροσβεστική]

✈ Dial 199 or 100.

fire extinguisher o pirosvestiras [ο πυροσβεστήρας]
first protos [πρώτος]

I was first *(said by man/woman)* ego imoon protos/proti [εγώ ήμουν πρώτος/πρώτη]
first aid protes vo-ITHi-es [πρώτες βοήθειες]
first aid kit ta efothia proton vo-ITHion [τα εφόδια πρώτων βοηθειών]
first class *(travel)* proti THesi [πρώτη θέση]
first name to onoma [το όνομα]
fish to psari [το ψάρι]
fishing to psarema [το ψάρεμα]
fit *(healthy)* iyiis [υγιής]
(physically) yimnasmenos [γυμνασμένος]
it doesn't fit me then moo KHora-i [δεν μου χωράει]
fix: can you fix it? *(repair)* boriteh na to thiorTHoseteh? [μπορείτε να το διορθώσετε;]
fizzy meh anTHrakiko [με ανθρακικό]
flag i simea [η σημαία]
flash *(photography)* to flas [το φλας]
flat *(adjective)* epipethos [επίπεδος]
(apartment) to thiamerisma [το διαμέρισμα]
I've got a flat (tyre) mepiaseh lastiKHo [μ'έπιασε λάστιχο]
flavour i yefsi [η γεύση]
flea enas psilos [ένας ψύλλος]
flies *(on trousers)* to fermooar [το φερμουάρ]
flight i ptisi [η πτήση]
flight number o ariTHmos ptisis [ο αριθμός πτήσης]
flippers ta vatraKHopethila [τα βατραχοπέδιλα]
flirt *(verb)* flertaro [φλερτάρω]
float *(verb)* epipleo [επιπλέω]
floor *(ground)* to patoma [το πάτωμα]
on the second floor sto theftero patoma [στο δεύτερο πάτωμα]
flower ena looloothi [ένα λουλούδι]
flu i gripi [η γρίππη]
fly *(insect)* mia miga [μιά μύγα]

(verb: go by plane) pao a-eroporikos [πάω αεροπορικώς]
foggy omikHlothis [ομιχλώδης]
follow akolooTHo [ακολουθώ]
food to fayito [το φαγητό]
(groceries) ithi pandopolioo [είδη παντοπωλείου]
we'd like to eat Greek-style food THa THelameh na thokimasoomeh eliniko fayito [θα θέλαμε να δοκιμάσουμε ελληνικό φαγητό]
food poisoning i trofiki thilitiriasi [η τροφική δηλητηρίαση]
fool enas ano-itos [ένας ανόητος]
(woman) mia ano-iti [μιά ανόητη]
foot to pothi [το πόδι]

✈ 1 foot = 30.5 cm = 0.3 metres

football *(game)* to pothosfero [το ποδόσφαιρο]
(ball) i bala too pothosferoo [η μπάλλα του ποδοσφαίρου]
for ya [για]
that's for me ya mena [για μένα]
forbidden apagorevmenos [απαγορευμένος]
foreign ksenos [ξένος]
foreign currency to kseno sinalagma [το ξένο συνάλλαγμα]
foreigner o ksenos [ο ξένος]
(woman) i kseni [η ξένη]
forest to thasos [το δάσος]
forget ksekHno [ξεχνώ]
I forget ksekHno [ξεχνώ]
I've forgotten ksekHasa [ξέχασα]
don't forget min ksekHasis [μην ξεχάσεις]
fork *(to eat with)* ena pirooni [ένα πηρούνι]
form *(document)* ena endipo [ένα έντυπο]
formal episimos [επίσημος]
(person) tipikos [τυπικός]
fortnight thio evthomathes [δύο εβδομάδες]

forward *(move etc)* brosta [μπροστά]
could you forward my mail? boriteh na metavivaseteh ta gramata moo? [μπορείτε να μεταβιβάσετε τα γράμματά μου;]
forwarding address i thi-efTHinsi apostolis [η διεύθυνση αποστολής]
foundation cream mia krema prosopoo os vasi [μιά κρέμα προσώπου ως βάση]
fountain mia piyi [μιά πηγή]
four-wheel drive ena tzip [ένα τζιπ]
fracture ena katagma [ένα κάταγμα]
fragile efTHrafstos [εύθραυστος]
France i galia [η Γαλλία]
fraud mia apati [μιά απάτη]
free eleftHeros [ελεύθερος]
(no charge) thorean [δωρεάν]
admission free eleftHera isothos [ελευθέρα είσοδος]
freight to fortio [το φορτίο]
French galikos [Γαλλικός]
fresh freskos [φρέσκος]
freshen up: I'd like to freshen up THelo na freskaristo [θέλω να φρεσκαριστώ]
Friday paraskevi [Παρασκευή]
fridge to psiyio [το ψυγείο]
fried egg ena avgo tiganito [ένα αυγό τηγανιτό]
friend enas filos [ένας φίλος]
(female) mia fili [μιά φίλη]
friendly filikos [φιλικός]
fries i patates tiganites [οι πατάτες τηγανητές]
from apo [από]
where is it from? apo poo ineh? [από πού είναι;]
front: in front of you brosta soo [μπροστά σου]
at the front brosta [μπροστά]
fruit to frooto [το φρούτο]
fruit salad mia frootosalata [μιά φρουτοσαλάτα]

fry tiganizo [τηγανίζω]
  nothing fried tipota tiganito [τίποτα τηγανιτό]
frying pan to tigani [το τηγάνι]
full yematos [γεμάτος]
fun: it's fun ineh thiaskethastiko [είναι διασκεδαστικό]
  have fun! kali thiaskethasi [καλή διασκέδαση]
funny *(strange)* peri-ergos [περίεργος]
  (comical) astios [αστείος]
furniture ta epipla [τα έπιπλα]
further parapera [παραπέρα]
fuse i asfalia [η ασφάλεια]
future: in the future sto melon [στο μέλλον]

G

gale mia THi-ela [μιά θύελλα]
gallon ena galoni [ένα γαλόνι]

> ✈ 1 gallon = 4.55 litres

gallstone mia petra tis KHolis [μιά πέτρα της χολής]
gamble pezo tiKHera peKHnithia [παίζω τυχερά παιχνίδια]
garage *(for repairs)* to sineryio [το συνεργείο]
  (for petrol) to venzinathiko [το βενζινάδικο]
  (for parking) to garaz [το γκαράζ]

> ✈ Usually open from around 8 am to 8 pm. Buying petrol at night and at weekends may not be easy; a list of garages open will usually be available on a garage door.

garden o kipos [ο κήπος]
garlic to skortho [το σκόρδο]
gas to gazi [το γκάζι]
  (petrol) i venzini [η βενζίνη]
gas cylinder mia fiali a-erioo [μιά φιάλη αερίου]

gasket i flantza [η φλάντζα]
gay 'gay' [γκέι]
gear *(in car)* i taKHitita [η ταχύτητα]
(equipment) ta ergalia [τα εργαλεία]
I can't get it into gear then boro na valo taKHitita [δεν μπορώ να βάλω ταχύτητα]
gents i tooaleta [η τουαλέτα]
German yermanikos [Γερμανικός]
Germany i yermania [η Γερμανία]
gesture i KHironomia [η χειρονομία]

✈ An outstretched open palm is a rude gesture in Greece.

get: will you get me a...? moo ferneteh ena...? [μου φέρνετε ένα...;]
how do I get to...? pos boro na pao sto...? [πώς μπορώ να πάω στο...;]
where do I get a bus for...? apo poo na paro to leoforio ya...? [από πού να πάρω το λεοφωρείο για...;]
when can I get it back? poteh boro na to paro piso? [πότε μπορώ να το πάρω πίσω;]
when do we get back? poteh yirizoomeh? [πότε γυρίζουμε;]
where do I get off? poo na katevo? [πού να κατέβω;]
have you got...? eKHeteh...? [έχετε...;]
(familiar) eKHis...? [έχεις...;]
gin ena tzin [ένα τζιν]
gin and tonic ena tzin meh tonik [ένα τζιν με τόνικ]
girl ena koritsi [ένα κορίτσι]
girlfriend i filenatha [η φιλενάδα]
give thino [δίνω]
will you give me...? moo thineteh...? [μου δίνετε...;]
I gave it to him too to ethosa [του το έδωσα]

glad efkHaristimenos [ευχαριστημένος]
I'm glad kHeromeh [χαίρομαι]
glass to yali [το γυαλί]
(drinking) ena potiri [ένα ποτήρι]
a glass of water ena potiri nero [ένα ποτήρι νερό]
glasses ta yalia [τα γυαλιά]
glue i kola [η κόλλα]
go piyeno [πηγαίνω]
I want to go to Delphi tHelo na pao stoos thelfoos [θέλω να πάω στους Δελφούς]
when does the bus go? poteh tHa fiyi to leoforio? [πότε θα φύγει το λεωφορείο;]
the bus has gone to leoforio efiyeh [το λεωφορείο έφυγε]
he's gone efiyeh [έφυγε]
where are you going? poo pas? [πού πας;]
let's go pameh [πάμε]
go on! sinekHiseh! [συνέχισε!]
can I have a go? boro na prospatHiso? [μπορώ να προσπαθήσω;]
goal ena gol [ένα γκολ]
goat's cheese to katsikisio tiri [το κατσικίσιο τυρί]
god o tHeos [ο θεός]
goddess i tHea [η θεά]
gold o kHrisos [ο χρυσός]
golf to golf [το γκολφ]
good kalos [καλός]
good! kala! [καλά!]
goodbye yasoo [γειά σου]

> **Yasoo** also means 'hello'.

got: have you got...? ekHeteh...? [έχετε...;]
(familiar) ekHis...? [έχεις...;]
gram to gramario [το γραμμάριο]
granddaughter i engoni [η εγγονή]
grandfather o papoos [ο παππούς]

grandmother i yaya [η γιαγιά]
grandson o engonos [ο εγγονός]
grapefruit ena 'grapefruit' [ένα γκρέιπφρουτ]
grapefruit juice enas KHimos apo 'grapefruit' [ένας χυμός από γκρέιπφρουτ]
grapes ta stafilia [τα σταφύλια]
grass to KHortari [το χορτάρι]
grateful: I'm very grateful to you sas imeh efgnomon [σας είμαι ευγνώμων]
gravy i saltsa [η σάλτσα]
grease to graso [το γράσσο]
greasy liparos [λιπαρός]
great megalos [μεγάλος]
(very good) iperoKHos [υπέροχος]
great! THavmasia! [θαυμάσια!]
Greece i elatha [η Ελλάδα]
in ancient Greece stin arKHeh-a elatha [στην Αρχαία Ελλάδα]
greedy aplistos [άπληστος]
(for food) aKHortagos [αχόρταγος]
Greek *(adjective)* elinikos [Ελληνικός]
(man) o elinas [ο Έλληνας]
(woman) i elinitha [η Ελληνίδα]
(language) ta elinika [τα Ελληνικά]
the Greeks i elines [οι Έλληνες]
green prasinos [πράσινος]
grey grizos [γκρίζος]
grocer's to pandopolio [το παντοπωλείο]
ground to ethafos [το έδαφος]
on the ground floor sto isoyio [στο ισόγειο]
group i omatha [η ομάδα]
our group leader o/i arKHigos tis omathas mas [ο/η αρχηγός της ομάδας μας]
I'm with the English group imeh meh tin angliki omatha [είμαι με την Αγγλική ομάδα]
guarantee mia engi-isi [μιά εγγύηση]
guest enas filoksenoomenos

[ένας φιλοξενούμενος]
(woman) mia filoksenoomeni [μιά φιλοξενούμενη]
(in hotel) enas/mia pelatis [ένας/μιά πελάτης]
guesthouse i pansion [η πανσιόν]
guide o/i ksenagos [ο/η ξεναγός]
guidebook enas tooristikos othigos [ένας τουριστικός οδηγός]
guided tour mia xena-yisi [μιά ξενάγηση]
guilty enoKHos [ένοχος]
guitar i kiTHara [η κιθάρα]
gum *(in mouth)* to oolo [το ούλο]
gun *(rifle)* to oplo [το όπλο]
(pistol) to pistoli [το πιστόλι]

H

hair ta malia [τα μαλλιά]
haircut ena koorema [ένα κούρεμα]
hairdresser's to komotirio [το κομμωτήριο]
is there a hairdresser's here? iparKHi komotirio etho? [υπάρχει κομμωτήριο εδώ;]
hair grip ena piastraki ya ta malia [ένα πιαστράκι για τα μαλλιά]
half misos [μισός]
a half portion misi meritha [μισή μερίδα]
half an hour misi ora [μισή ώρα]
go to **time**
ham to KHirino [το χοιρινό]
hamburger ena KHamboorger [ένα χάμπουργκερ]
hammer ena sfiri [ένα σφυρί]
hand to KHeri [το χέρι]
handbag i tsanda [η τσάντα]
hand baggage to sak-vooayaz [το σακ-βουαγιαζ]
handbrake to KHirofreno [το χειρόφρενο]
handkerchief ena mandili [ένα μαντήλι]
handle to KHerooli [το χερούλι]
handmade KHiropi-itos [χειροποίητος]

handsome oreos [ωραίος]
hanger mia kremastra [μιά κρεμάστρα]
hangover: I've got a terrible hangover eKHo fovero ponokefalo meta to KHtesino meTHisi [έχω φοβερό πονοκέφαλο μετά το χτεσινό μεθύσι]
happen simveni [συμβαίνει]
I don't know how it happened then ksero pos sinevi [δεν ξέρω πώς συνέβη]
what's happening? ti simveni? [τί συμβαίνει;]
what's happened? ti sinevi? [τί συνέβη;]
happy eftiKHismenos [ευτυχισμένος]
harbour to limani [το λιμάνι]
hard skliros [σκληρός]
(difficult) thiskolos [δύσκολος]
hard-boiled egg ena sfikto avgo [ένα σφικτό αυγό]
harm i zimia [η ζημιά]
hat to kapelo [το καπέλο]
hate: I hate... miso... [μισώ...]
have eKHo [έχω]
can I have...? boro na eKHo...? [μπορώ να έχω...;]
I have no... then eKHo... [δεν έχω...]
do you have any cigars/a map? eKHeteh poora/enan KHarti? [έχετε πούρα/έναν χάρτη;]
I have to leave tomorrow *prepi na* figo avrio [πρέπει να φύγω αύριο]

Here is the present tense of the verb 'to have'.

I have eKHo [έχω]
you have *(familiar singular)* eKHis [έχεις]
he/she/it has eKHi [έχει]
we have eKHoomeh [έχουμε]
you have *(polite or plural)* eKHeteh [έχετε]
they have eKHoon [έχουν]

hay fever o aleryikos piretos [ο αλλεργικός πυρετός]
he aftos [αυτός]

> If there is no special emphasis Greek doesn't use the word **aftos**.
> **where does he live?** poo meni? [πού μένει;]

head to kefali [το κεφάλι]
headache enas ponokefalos [ένας πονοκέφαλος]
headlight o faros [ο φάρος]

> ✈ If a driver flashes his headlights at you, this will mean 'look out' and not 'after you'.

head waiter o arkHiservitoros [ο αρχισερβιτόρος]
head wind enas andiTHetos anemos [ένας αντίθετος άνεμος]
health i iyia [η υγεία]
your health! stin iya soo [στην υγειά σου]
hear: I can't hear then boro na *akooso* [δεν μπορώ να ακούσω]
hearing aid ta akoostika [τα ακουστικά]
heart i karthia [η καρδιά]
heart attack mia karthiaki prosvoli [μιά καρδιακή προσβολή]
heat i zesti [η ζέστη]
heating i THermansi [η θέρμανση]
heat stroke i iliasi [η ηλίαση]
heavy varis [βαρύς]
heel i fterna [η φτέρνα]
(of shoe) to takooni [το τακούνι]
could you put new heels on these? boriteh na valeteh kenoorya takoonia seh afta? [μπορείτε να βάλετε καινούρια τακούνια σε αυτά;]
height to ipsos [το ύψος]
hello yasoo [γειά σου]
(on phone) embros [εμπρός]

> **Yasoo** also means 'goodbye'.

help i vo-iTHia [η βοήθεια]
can you help me? boriteh na meh vo-iTHiseteh? [μπορείτε να με βοηθήσετε;]
help! vo-iTHia! [βοήθεια!]
her[1] afti [αυτή]
I know her tin ksero afti [την ξέρω αυτή]
will you give it to her? THa *tis* to thosis? [θα της το δώσεις;]
with her mazi tis [μαζί της]
it's her afti ineh [αυτή είναι]
who? – her pios? – afti [ποιός; – αυτή]
her[2] *(possessive)*

> To say 'her...' you wrap the Greek for 'the' (either of **o/i/to**) and the word **tis** around what is hers.
> **her hotel** to ksenothoKHio tis [το ξενοδοχείο της]

here etho [εδώ]
come here ela etho [έλα εδώ]
hers: it's hers ineh thikos tis [είναι δικός της]
hi! yasoo [γειά σου]
high psila [ψηλά]
higher up psilotera [ψηλότερα]
high chair ena kareklaki moroo [ένα καρεκλάκι μωρού]
hill o lofos [ο λόφος]
(on road) to ipsoma [το ύψωμα]
it's up/down the hill ineh eki pano/eki kato [είναι εκεί πάνω/εκεί κάτω]
him: I don't know him then *ton* ksero [δεν τον ξέρω]
will you give it to him? THa *too* to thosis? [θα του το δώσεις;]
with him mazi too [μαζί του]

for him yafton [γι' αυτόν]
it's him *aftos* ineh [αυτός είναι]
who? – him pios? – aftos [ποιός; – αυτός]
hire *go to* **rent**
his

> To say 'his...' you wrap the Greek for 'the' (either of **o/i/to**) and the word **too** around what is his.
> **his bag** i tsanda too [η τσάντα του]
> **it's his** ineh thikos too [είναι δικός του]

hit: he hit me meh ktipiseh [με κτύπησε]
hitch-hike kano oto-stop [κάνω ότο-στοπ]
hitch-hiking to oto-stop [το ότο-στοπ]
hold *(verb)* krato [κρατώ]
hole mia tripa [μιά τρύπα]
holiday i thiakopes [οι διακοπές]
(single day) mia aryia [μιά αργία]
I'm on holiday kano thiakopes [κάνω διακοπές]
Holland i olanthia [η Ολλανδία]
home to spiti [το σπίτι]
at home sto spiti [στο σπίτι]
(back in Britain) sti vretania [στη Βρεταννία]
I want to go home THelo na pao spiti [θέλω να πάω σπίτι]
homesick: I'm homesick nostalgo to spiti moo [νοσταλγώ το σπίτι μου]
honest timios [τίμιος]
honestly? logo timis? [λόγω τιμής;]
honey to meli [το μέλι]
honeymoon o minas too melitos [ο μήνας του μέλιτος]
hope i elpitha [η ελπίδα]
I hope that... elpizo oti... [ελπίζω ότι...]
I hope so elpizo pos neh [ελπίζω πως ναι]
I hope not elpizo pos oKHi [ελπίζω πως όχι]
horn *(of car)* to klakson [το κλάξον]

horrible apesios [απαίσιος]
horse to alogo [το άλογο]
hospital to nosokomio [το νοσοκομείο]

→ *go to* **doctor**

host o ikothespotis [ο οικοδεσπότης]
hostess i ikothespina [η οικοδέσποινα]
hot zestos [ζεστός]
(spiced) pikandikos [πικάντικος]
I'm so hot! zestenomeh para poli! [ζεσταίνομαι πάρα πολύ!]
it's so hot today! kani tosi zesti simera! [κάνει τόση ζέστη σήμερα!]
hotel to ksenothoKHio [το ξενοδοχείο]
at my hotel sto ksenothoKHio moo [στο ξενοδοχείο μου]
hour i ora [η ώρα]
house to spiti [το σπίτι]
how pos [πώς]
how many? posi? [πόσοι;]
how much? posa? [πόσα;]
how much is it? poso kani afto? [πόσο κάνει αυτό;]
how long does it take? posi ora kani? [πόση ώρα κάνει;]
how long have you been here? poso kero isteh etho? [πόσο καιρό είστε εδώ;]
how are you? ti kanis? [τί κάνεις;]
(polite form) ti kaneteh? [τί κάνετε;]

YOU MAY THEN HEAR
poli kala *very well*
etsi ki etsi *so-so*

hull to skari [το σκαρί]
humid igros [υγρός]
hungry: I'm hungry pinao [πεινάω]
I'm not hungry then pinao [δεν πεινάω]

hurry: I'm in a hurry viazomeh [βιάζομαι]
please hurry! grigora, parakalo! [γρήγορα, παρακαλώ!]
hurt: it hurts pona-i [πονάει]
my leg hurts pona-i to pothi moo [πονάει το πόδι μου]
husband o sizigos [ο σύζυγος]

I

I ego [εγώ]

> If there is no special emphasis Greek doesn't use the word **ego**.
> **I am a doctor** imeh yatros [είμαι γιατρός]

ice o pagos [ο πάγος]
with lots of ice meh poli pago [με πολύ πάγο]
ice cream ena pagoto [ένα παγωτό]
iced coffee enas kafes frapeh meh pago [ένας καφές φραπέ με πάγο]
identity papers i taftotita [η ταυτότητα]
idiot enas vlakas [ένας βλάκας]
if an [αν]
ignition *(of car)* i miza [η μίζα]
ill arostos [άρρωστος]
I feel ill esTHanomeh asKHima [αισθάνομαι άσχημα]
illegal paranomos [παράνομος]
illegible thisanagnostos [δυσανάγνωστος]
illness mia arostia [μιά αρρώστεια]
immediately amesos [αμέσως]
important *(person)* spootheos [σπουδαίος]
it's very important ineh poli simandiko [είναι πολύ σημαντικό]
impossible athinato [αδύνατο]
impressive endiposiakos [εντυπωσιακός]
improve veltiono [βελτιώνω]

I want to improve my Greek THelo na veltioso ta elinika moo [θέλω να βελτιώσω τα ελληνικά μου]
in sto [στο]
in London sto lonthino [στο Λονδίνο]
in England stin anglia [στην Αγγλία]
is he in? ineh mesa? [είναι μέσα;]
inch mia intsa [μιά ίντσα]

✈ 1 inch = 2.54 cm

include perilamvano [περιλαμβάνω]
does that include breakfast? afto perilamvani keh pro-ino? [αυτό περιλαμβάνει και πρωινό;]
incompetent anikanos [ανίκανος]
inconsiderate aperiskeptos [απερίσκεπτος]
incredible apisteftos [απίστευτος]
indecent aprepis [απρεπής]
independent aneksartitos [ανεξάρτητος]
India i inthia [η Ινδία]
indicate: he turned without indicating estripseh KHoris na kani sima [έστριψε χωρίς να κάνει σήμα]
indicator *(on car)* o thiktis porias [ο δείκτης πορείας]
indigestion i thispepsia [η δυσπεψία]
indoors mesa [μέσα]
infection mia molinsi [μιά μόλυνση]
infectious kolitikos [κολλητικός]
information i plirofori-es [οι πληροφορίες]
do you have any information in English about...? mipos eKHeteh plirofori-es sta anglika ya...? [μήπως έχετε πληροφορίες στα Αγγλικά για...;]
is there an information office? iparKHi grafio pliroforion? [υπάρχει γραφείο πληροφοριών;]
injection mia enesi [μιά ένεση]
injured travmatismenos [τραυματισμένος]

injury to travma [το τραύμα]
innocent aTHo-os [αθώος]
insect ena zo-ifio [ένα ζωύφιο]
insect repellent ena endomoktono [ένα εντομοκτόνο]
inside mesa [μέσα]
insist: I insist epimeno [επιμένω]
insomnia i a-ipnia [η αϋπνία]
instant coffee enas nes kafeh [ένας νες καφέ]
instead andi [αντί]
instead of... andi... [αντί...]
insulating tape mia monotiki tenia [μιά μονωτική ταινία]
insult i prosvoli [η προσβολή]
insurance i asfalia [η ασφάλεια]
insurance company i asfalistiki eteria [η ασφαλιστική εταιρεία]
intelligent eksipnos [έξυπνος]
interesting enthiaferon [ενδιαφέρων]
international thi-eTHnis [διεθνής]
Internet to thiathiktio [το διαδίκτυο]
Internet café ena internet kafeh [ένα 'Internet café']
interpret thi-erminevo [διερμηνεύω]
would you interpret for us? boriteh na isteh o thi-ermineas mas? [μπορείτε να είστε ο διερμηνέας μας;]
interpreter enas/mia thi-ermineas [ένας/μιά διερμηνέας]
into mesa [μέσα]
I'm not into that *(don't like)* then moo aresoon afta [δεν μου αρέσουν αυτά]
introduce: can I introduce...? na sas sistiso? apo etho... [να σας συστήσω; από εδώ...]
invalid *(disabled)* enas anapiros [ένας ανάπηρος]
(woman) mia anapiri [μιά ανάπηρη]
invitation mia prosklisi [μιά πρόσκληση]

thanks for the invitation efkHaristo ya tin prosklisi [ευχαριστώ για την πρόσκληση]

✈ Customary to bring a present of sweets or flowers for your host. In many places hospitality is still a matter of honour: for this reason, avoid offending your hosts by being unwilling to eat what you are served.

invite: can I invite you out? boro na sas *proskaleso* na vgoomeh ekso? [μπορώ να σας προσκαλέσω να βγούμε έξω;]
Ireland i irlanthia [η Ιρλανδία]
Irish irlanthikos [Ιρλανδικός]
Irishman o irlanthos [ο Ιρλανδός]
Irishwoman i irlantheza [η Ιρλανδέζα]
iron *(for clothes)* ena ilektriko sithero [ένα ηλεκτρικό σίδερο]
will you iron these for me? boriteh na moo sitheroseteh afta? [μπορείτε να μου σιδερώσετε αυτά;]
is *go to* **be**
island to nisi [το νησί]
we're island-hopping taksithevoomeh apo to ena nisi sto alo [ταξιδεύουμε από το ένα νησί στο άλλο]
it afto [αυτό]
put it here valeh *to* etho [βάλε το εδώ]
I'll take it THa to paro [θα το πάρω]

If there is no special emphasis Greek doesn't use the word **afto** as a subject.
it is ineh [είναι]
it's not working then litooryi [δεν λειτουργεί]

Italy i italia [η Ιταλία]
itch: it itches eKHo fagoora [έχω φαγούρα]
itemize: would you itemize it for me? boriteh

na moo kaneteh ton logariasmo ya kaTHeh ti KHorista? [μπορείτε να μου κάνετε τον λογαριασμό για κάθε τι χωριστά;]

J

jack *(for car)* o grilos [ο γρύλος]
jacket ena sakaki [ένα σακάκι]
jam i marmelatha [η μαρμελάδα]
traffic jam ena botiliarisma [ένα μποτιλιάρισμα]
January ianooarios [Ιανουάριος]
jaw to sagoni [το σαγόνι]
jealous ziliaris [ζηλιάρης]
jeans ta tzins [τα τζηνς]
jeep ena tzip [ένα τζιπ]
jellyfish mia tsooKHtra [μιά τσούχτρα]
jetty o molos [ο μώλος]
jewellery ta kosmimata [τα κοσμήματα]
job mia thoolia [μιά δουλειά]
just the job akrivos afto [ακριβώς αυτό]
joke ena astio [ένα αστείο]
you must be joking! asti-eveseh sigoora! [αστειεύεσαι σίγουρα!]
journey to taksithi [το ταξίδι]
have a good journey! kalo taksithi [καλό ταξίδι]
July ioolios [Ιούλιος]
junction i thiastavrosi [η διασταύρωση]
June ioonios [Ιούνιος]
junk i koorelari-es [οι κουρελαρίες]
(food) plastiki trofi [πλαστική τροφή]
just *(only)* mono [μόνο]
(exactly) akrivos [ακριβώς]
just a little ligo mono [λίγο μόνο]
not just now oKHi tora amesos [όχι τώρα μέσως]
he was here just now itan etho molis tora

[ήταν εδώ μόλις τώρα]
that's just right afto ineh oti prepi [αυτό είναι ότι πρέπει]

K

kebab ena soovlaki yiros [ένα σουβλάκι γύρος]
keep: can I keep it? boro na to kratiso? [μπορώ να το κρατήσω;]
you keep it parto esi [πάρ'το εσύ]
keep the change krata ta resta [κράτα τα ρέστα]
you didn't keep your promise then kratises tin iposkHesi soo [δεν κράτησες την υπόσχεσή σου]
it keeps on breaking spa-i sinekHos [σπάει συνεχώς]
key to klithi [το κλειδί]
keycard mia karta analipseon [μιά κάρτα αναλήψεων]
kidneys ta nefra [τα νεφρά]
kill skotono [σκοτώνω]
kilo ena kilo [ένα κιλό]

✈ kilos/5 x 11 = pounds

kilos	1	1.5	5	6	7	8	9
pounds	2.2	3.3	11	13.2	15.4	17.6	19.8

kilometre ena kHiliometro [ένα χιλιόμετρο]

✈ kms/8 x 5 = miles

kilometres	1	5	10	20	50	100
miles	0.62	3.11	6.2	12.4	31	62

kind: that's very kind of you afto ineh poli *evyeniko* ek meroos sas [αυτό είναι πολύ ευγενικό εκ μέρους σας]
what kind of...? ti ithos...? [τί είδος...;]
kiosk to periptero [το περίπτερο]

✈ Kiosks sell tobacco, magazines, chocolate, soft drinks etc; they also have telephones and sell stamps and phonecards.

kiss ena fili [ένα φιλί]
(verb) filao [φιλάω]

✈ Normal amongst Greeks to greet friends and relatives by kissing them on both cheeks. Men shake hands instead.

kitchen i koozina [η κουζίνα]
knee to gonato [το γόνατο]
knife ena maKHeri [ένα μαχαίρι]
knock *(at door)* KHtipo [χτυπώ]
there's a knocking noise from the engine akooyeteh enas ktipos apo ti miKHani [ακούγεται ένας κτύπος από τη μηχανή]
know ksero [ξέρω]
(person, place) gnorizo [γνωρίζω]
I don't know then ksero [δεν ξέρω]
I didn't know then to iksera [δεν το ήξερα]

L

label i etiketa [η ετικέτα]
laces ta korthonia [τα κορδόνια]
lacquer i lak [η λακ]
ladies *(toilet)* i tooaleta [η τουαλέτα]
lady mia kiria [μιά κυρία]
lager mia bira [μιά μπύρα]
a lager and lime mia bira meh 'lime' [μιά μπύρα με λάιμ]

✈ This is an unusual drink in Greece.

lake i limni [η λίμνη]
lamb *(meat)* to arni [το αρνί]
lamp i lamba [η λάμπα]

lamppost o stilos ilektrikoo [ο στύλος ηλεκτρικού]
lampshade ena ambazoor [ένα αμπαζούρ]
land i yi [η γη]
lane *(on road)* i loritha [η λωρίδα]
language i glosa [η γλώσσα]
language course ta maTHimata ksenis glosas [τα μαθήματα ξένης γλώσσας]
laptop enas foritos ipolo-yistis [ένας φορητός υπολογιστής]
large megalos [μεγάλος]
laryngitis i laringititha [η λαρυγγίτιδα]
last telefteos [τελευταίος]
last year perisi [πέρυσι]
last week tin perasmeni evthomatha [την περασμένη εβδομάδα]
last night KHTHes vrathi [χθες βράδυ]
at last! epiteloos! [επιτέλους!]
late arga [αργά]
sorry I'm late meh sinKHoriteh poo aryisa [με συγχωρείτε που άργησα]
it's a bit late ineh kapos arga [είναι κάπως αργά]
please hurry, I'm late pio grigora parakalo, eKHo aryisi [πιό γρήγορα παρακαλώ, έχω αργήσει]
at the latest to argotero [το αργότερο]
later argotera [αργότερα]
see you later THa ta ksanapoomeh [θα τα ξαναπούμε]
laugh *(verb)* yelo [γελώ]
launderette to plintirio [το πλυντήριο]

> ✈ These are rare. But most rooms to rent will have washing facilities.

lavatory i tooaleta [η τουαλέτα]
law o nomos [ο νόμος]
lawyer o/i thikigoros [ο/η δικηγόρος]
laxative ena kaTHarsio [ένα καθάρσιο]
lay-by to parkin [το πάρκιν]

lazy tembelis [τεμπέλης]
leaf to filo [το φύλλο]
leak i thiaro-i [η διαρροή]
it leaks stazi [στάζει]
learn: I want to learn... THelo na maTHO... [θέλω να μάθω...]
lease nikiazo [νοικιάζω]
least: not in the least kaTHoloo [καθόλου]
at least toolakHiston [τουλάχιστον]
leather to therma [το δέρμα]
leave *(go away)* fevgo [φεύγω]
we're leaving tomorrow fevgoomeh avrio [φεύγουμε αύριο]
when does the bus leave? poteh fevyi to leoforio? [πότε φεύγει το λεωφορείο;]
I left two shirts in my room *afisa* thio pookamisa sto thomatio moo [άφησα δύο πουκάμισα στο δωμάτιό μου]
can I leave this here? boro nafiso afto etho? [μπορώ ν'αφήσω αυτό εδώ;]
left aristera [αριστερά]
on the left pros taristera [προς τ'αριστερά]
left-handed aristerokHiras [αριστερόχειρας]
left luggage (office) o kHoros filaksis aposkevon [ο χώρος φύλαξης αποσκευών]
leg to pothi [το πόδι]
legal *(permitted)* nominos [νόμιμος]
lemon ena lemoni [ένα λεμόνι]
lemonade mia lemonatha [μιά λεμονάδα]
lend: will you lend me...? boris na moo thanisis...? [μπορείς να μου δανείσεις...;]
lens o fakos [ο φακός]
Lent i sarakosti [η Σαρακοστή]
less ligoteros [λιγότερος]
less than that ligotero apo ekino [λιγότερο από εκείνο]
let: let me help aseh meh na seh vo-iTHiso [άσε με

να σε βοηθήσω]
let me go! aseh meh na figo [άσε με να φύγω]
will you let me off here? THa meh afisis na katevo etho? [θα με αφήσεις να κατέβω εδώ;]
let's go pameh! [πάμε!]
letter ena grama [ένα γράμμα]
are there any letters for me? eKHo kanena grama? [έχω κανένα γράμμα;]
letterbox ena taKHithromiko kooti [ένα ταχυδρομικό κουτί]

✈ Usually bright yellow.

YOU MAY SEE
ΕΣΩΤΕΡΙΚΟΥ *inland*
ΕΞΩΤΕΡΙΚΟΥ *overseas*

lettuce ena marooli [ένα μαρούλι]
level-crossing i isopethi thiavasi [η ισόπεδη διάβαση]
liable *(responsible)* ipefTHinos [υπεύθυνος]
library i vivlioTHiki [η βιβλιοθήκη]
licence mia athia [μιά άδεια]
lid to kapaki [το καπάκι]
lie *(untruth)* ena psema [ένα ψέμα]
can he lie down for a bit? bori na ksaplosi ya ligo? [μπορεί να ξαπλώσει για λίγο;]
life i zo-i [η ζωή]
that's life etsi ineh i zo-i [έτσι είναι η ζωή]
lifebelt to sosivio [το σωσίβιο]
lifeboat i sosivia lemvos [η σωσίβια λέμβος]
life-guard o navagosostis [ο ναυαγοσώστης]
life insurance mia asfalia zo-is [μιά ασφάλεια ζωής]
life jacket to sosivio [το σωσίβιο]
lift: do you want a lift? THeleteh na sas paro mazi moo? [θέλετε να σας πάρω μαζί μου;]
could you give me a lift? boriteh na meh pareteh mazi sas? [μπορείτε να με πάρετε μαζί

σας;]

the lift isn't working o *anelkistiras* then thoolevi [ο ανελκυστήρας δεν δουλεύει]

light *(not heavy)* elafros [ελαφρός]

(not dark) anikHtokHromos [ανοιχτόχρωμος]

the light to fos [το φως]

the lights aren't working ta fota then anavoon [τα φώτα δεν ανάβουν]

have you got a light? ekHis fotia? [έχεις φωτιά;]

light red anikHtos [ανοιχτός]

light bulb enas glombos [ένας γλόμπος]

lighter enas anaptiras [ένας αναπτήρας]

like: would you like...? THa THelateh...? [θα θέλατε...;]

(familiar) THelis...? [θέλεις...;]

I'd like a... THa iTHela ena... [θα ήθελα ένα...]

I'd like to... THa iTHela na... [θα ήθελα να...]

I like it moo aresi [μου αρέσει]

I like you moo aresis [μου αρέσεις]

I don't like it then moo aresi [δεν μου αρέσει]

what's it like? meh ti miazi? [με τί μοιάζει;]

do it like this kaneh to etsi [κάνε το έτσι]

one like that ena san keh afto [ένα σαν και αυτό]

lime ena 'lime' [ένα λάιμ]

lime juice enas kHimos 'lime' [ένας χυμός λάιμ]

line mia grami [μιά γραμμή]

lip to kHili [το χείλι]

lip salve ena vootiro kakao [ένα βούτυρο κακάο]

lipstick ena krayon [ένα κραγιαν]

liqueur ena liker [ένα λικέρ]

list o katalogos [ο κατάλογος]

listen akoo-o [ακούω]

listen! akoo! [άκου!]

litre ena litro [ένα λίτρο]

✈ 1 litre = 1.75 pints = 0.22 gals

little mikros [μικρός]

a little ligo [λίγο]
a little ice ligo pago [λίγο πάγο]
a little more akomi ligo [ακόμη λίγο]
live zo [ζω]
I live in Glasgow meno sti glaskovi [μένω στη Γλασκώβη]
where do you live? poo menis? [πού μένεις;]
liver to sikoti [το συκώτι]
lizard i savra [η σαύρα]
loaf mia frantzola [μιά φραντζόλα]
lobster enas astakos [ένας αστακός]
local: could we try a local wine? boroomeh na thokimasoomeh ena *dopio* krasi? [μπορούμε να δοκιμάσουμε ένα ντόπιο κρασί;]
a local restaurant ena estiatorio *tis perioKHis* [ένα εστιατόριο της περιοχής]
lock: the lock's broken i klitharia ineh spasmeni [η κλειδαριά είναι σπασμένη]
I've locked myself out klithoTHika ekso [κλειδώθηκα έξω]
London to lonthino [το Λονδίνο]
lonely *(person)* monaKHikos [μοναχικός]
long makris [μακρύς]
we'd like to stay longer THa THelameh na minoomeh perisotero [θα θέλαμε να μείνουμε περισσότερο]
a long time polis keros [πολύς καιρός]
loo: where's the loo? poo ineh i tooaleta? [πού είναι η τουαλέτα;]
look: you look tired feneseh koorasmenos/koorasmeni [φαίνεσαι κουρασμένος/κουρασμένη]
look at that kitakseh afto [κοίταξε αυτό]
can I have a look? boro na tho? [μπορώ να δω;]
I'm just looking apla vlepo [απλά βλέπω]
will you look after my bags? THa *proseKHis* tis valitses moo? [θα προσέχεις τις βαλίτσες μου;]
I'm looking for... psaKHno ya... [ψάχνω για...]

look out! prosekheh! [πρόσεχε!]
loose khalaros [χαλαρός]
lorry to fortigo [το φορτηγό]
lorry driver enas othigos fortigoo [ένας οδηγός φορτηγού]
lose khano [χάνω]
I've lost... ekhasa... [έχασα...]
excuse me, I'm lost meh sinkhoriteh, ekho khathi [με συγχωρείτε, έχω χαθεί]
lost property (office) ta apolesthenda [τα απολεσθέντα]
lot: a lot pola [πολλά]
not a lot okhi pola [όχι πολλά]
a lot of chips poles patates tiganites [πολλές πατάτες τηγανιτές]
a lot of wine poli krasi [πολύ κρασί]
a lot more expensive poli pio akrivo [πολύ πιό ακριβό]
lotion i losion [η λοσιόν]
loud *(noise)* thinatos [δυνατός]
louder pio thinata [πιό δυνατά]
it's too loud ineh poli thinata [είναι πολύ δυνατά]
lounge to saloni [το σαλόνι]
love: I love you sagapo [σ'αγαπώ]
do you love me? magapas? [μ'αγαπάς;]
he's/she's in love ineh erotevmenos/erotevmeni [είναι ερωτευμένος/ερωτευμένη]
I love this wine maresi afto to krasi [μ'αρέσει αυτό το κρασί]
lovely oreos [ωραίος]
low khamilos [χαμηλός]
luck i tikhi [η τύχη]
good luck! kali tikhi! [καλή τύχη!]
lucky tikheros [τυχερός]
that's lucky! afto ineh tikhero! [αυτό είναι τυχερό!]

luggage i aposkeves [οι αποσκευές]
lunch to yevma [το γεύμα]

✈ Greeks usually have a late lunch between 2 and 3 pm.

lungs i pnevmones [οι πνεύμονες]
luxury i politelia [η πολυτέλεια]

M

mad trelos [τρελλός]
made-to-measure rameno kata parangelia [ραμμένο κατά παραγγελία]
magazine ena periothiko [ένα περιοδικό]
magnificent megaloprepis [μεγαλοπρεπής]
maid i kamari-era [η καμαριέρα]
maiden name to patronimo [το πατρώνυμο]
mail ta gramata [τα γράμματα]
is there any mail for me? iparKHoon gramata ya mena? [υπάρχουν γράμματα για μένα;]
mainland: on the mainland sto esoteriko tis KHoras [στο εσωτερικό της χώρας]
main road o kendrikos thromos [ο κεντρικός δρόμος]
make kano [κάνω]
will we make it in time? THa prolavoomeh? [θα προλάβουμε;]
make-up to 'make-up' [το μέικ απ]
man o andras [ο άντρας]
manager o thiaKHiristis [ο διαχειριστής]
can I see the manager? boro na tho ton thiaKHiristi? [μπορώ να δω τον διαχειριστή;]
many poli [πολλοί]
map o KHartis [ο χάρτης]
a map of Athens enas KHartis tis aTHinas [ένας χάρτης της Αθήνας]
March martios [Μάρτιος]

marina i provlita [η προβλήτα]
market i agora [η αγορά]
marmalade i marmelatha [η μαρμελάδα]
married pandremenos [παντρεμένος]
marry: will you marry me? THa meh pandreftis? [θα με παντρευτείς;]
marvellous THavmasios [θαυμάσιος]
mascara i maskara [η μάσκαρα]
mashed potatoes patates pooreh [πατάτες πουρέ]
mass *(in church)* i litooryia [η λειτουργία]
massage ena masaz [ένα μασάζ]
mast to katarti [το κατάρτι]
mat ena KHalaki [ένα χαλάκι]
match: a box of matches ena kooti spirta [ένα κουτί σπίρτα]
a football match enas pothosferikos agonas [ένας ποδοσφαιρικός αγώνας]
material *(cloth)* to iliko [το υλικό]
matter: it doesn't matter then pirazi [δεν πειράζει]
what's the matter? ti simveni? [τί συμβαίνει;]
mattress to stroma [το στρώμα]
mature orimos [ώριμος]
maximum meyistos [μέγιστος]
May ma-ios [Μάιος]
may: may I have...? THa boroosa na eKHo...? [θα μπορούσα να έχω...;]
maybe bori [μπορεί]
mayonnaise i mayoneza [η μαγιονέζα]
me: he knows me meh gnorizi [με γνωρίζει]
give me... thoseh moo... [δώσε μου...]
with/from me memena/apo mena [μ'εμένα/από μένα]
it's for me ineh ya mena [είναι για μένα]
it's me ego imeh [εγώ είμαι]
who? – me pios? – ego [ποιός; – εγώ]
meal to yevma [το γεύμα]

mean: what does this mean? ti simeni afto? [τί σημαίνει αυτό;]
measles i ilara [η ιλαρά]
German measles i eriTHra [η ερυθρά]
measurements ta metra [τα μέτρα]
meat to kreas [το κρέας]
mechanic: is there a mechanic here? iparKHi kanenas miKHanikos etho? [υπάρχει κανένας μηχανικός εδώ;]
medicine to farmako [το φάρμακο]
Mediterranean i mesoyios [η Μεσόγειος]
meet sinando [συναντώ]
pleased to meet you KHeromeh poo sas gnorizo [χαίρομαι που σας γνωρίζω]
when shall we meet? poteh THa sinandiTHoomeh? [πότε θα συναντηθούμε;]
meeting i sinandisi [η συνάντηση]
melon ena peponi [ένα πεπόνι]
member ena melos [ένα μέλος]
how do I become a member? pos boro na yino melos? [πώς μπορώ να γίνω μέλος;]
men i andres [οι άντρες]
mend: can you mend this? boriteh na episkevaseteh afto? [μπορείτε να επισκευάσετε αυτό;]
mention: don't mention it! min to ksanapis! [μην το ξαναπείς!]
menu o katalogos [ο κατάλογος]
can I have the menu, please? boro na eKHo ton katalogo, parakalo? [μπορώ να έχω τον κατάλογο, παρακαλώ;]; *go to pages 80-83*
mess: it's a mess ineh ano kato [είναι άνω κάτω]
message ena minima [ένα μήνυμα]
are there any messages for me? iparKHi kanena minima ya mena? [υπάρχει κανένα μήνυμα για μένα;]
can I leave a message for...? boro na afiso ena minima ya...? [μπορώ να αφήσω ένα μήνυμα για...;]

I'd like
THa iTHela

can I have what he's having?
boro na eKHo afto poo pireh aftos?

water
nero

bread
psomi

red wine
kokino krasi

white wine
aspro krasi

ΟΡΕΚΤΙΚΑ orektika *starters*

ΝΤΟΛΜΑΔΑΚΙΑ ντολμαδάκια dolmathakia *vine leaves stuffed with minced meat, rice and herbs*

ΚΕΦΤΕΔΕΣ κεφτέδες keftethes *meat balls*

ΧΤΑΠΟΔΙ χταπόδι KHtapothi *octopus*

ΚΟΚΟΡΕΤΣΙ κοκορέτσι kokoretsi *spit-roasted liver and innards*

ΚΟΛΟΚΥΘΑΚΙΑ ΤΗΓΑΝΙΤΑ κολοκυθάκια τηγανιτά kolokiTHakia tiganita *fried baby marrows*

ΛΟΥΚΑΝΙΚΑ ΤΗΓΑΝΗΤΑ λουκάνικα τηγανητά lookanika tiganita *fried sausages*

ΜΕΛΙΤΖΑΝΟΣΑΛΑΤΑ μελιτζανοσαλάτα melitzanosalata *aubergine salad*

ΣΑΓΑΝΑΚΙ σαγανάκι saganaki *fried cheese*

ΣΑΛΑΤΑ ΧΩΡΙΑΤΙΚΗ σαλάτα χωριάτικη salata KHoriatiki *mixed salad*

ΣΠΑΝΑΚΟΠΙΤΑ σπανακόπιτα spanakopita *spinach squares*

ΤΑΡΑΜΟΣΑΛΑΤΑ ταραμοσαλάτα taramosalata *fish roe pâté*

ΤΖΑΤΖΙΚΙ τζατζίκι tzatziki *a mixture of cucumber, yogurt and garlic*

ΣΟΥΠΕΣ soopes *soups*

ΑΥΓΟΛΕΜΟΝΟ αυγολέμονο avgolemono *chicken broth, lemon and egg*

ΦΑΣΟΛΑΔΑ φασολάδα fasolatha *hot bean soup*

ΚΑΚΑΒΙΑ κακαβιά kakavia *various kinds of fish*

ΜΑΓΕΙΡΙΤΣΑ μαγειρίτσα mayiritsa *traditional lamb soup served on the Saturday night before Easter Sunday*

ΠΑΤΣΑΣ πατσάς patsas *lamb intestines thoroughly washed and cut up*

ΨΑΡΟΣΟΥΠΑ ψαρόσουπα psarosoopa *fish soup*

ΚΥΡΙΟ ΠΙΑΤΟ kirio piato *main course*

ΑΓΚΙΝΑΡΕΣ αγκινάρες aginares *artichokes in light sauce*

ΑΡΝΙ ΦΡΙΚΑΣΕ αρνί φρικασέ arni frikaseh *lamb, lettuce and thick white sauce*

ΜΠΙΦΤΕΚΙ μπιφτέκι bifteki *grilled meatballs*

ΜΠΡΙΖΟΛΕΣ ΧΟΙΡΙΝΕΣ μπριζόλες χοιρινές brizoles KHirines *pork chops*

ΝΤΟΜΑΤΕΣ ΓΕΜΙΣΤΕΣ ντομάτες γεμιστές domates yemistes *tomatoes with a stuffing of mince, rice and herbs*

ΓΑΡΙΔΟΠΙΛΑΦΟ γαριδοπίλαφο garithopilafo *prawns with rice cooked in butter*

ΚΛΕΦΤΙΚΟ κλέφτικο kleftiko *meat, potatoes and vegetables cooked together in a pot or foil*

ΚΟΤΑ ΨΗΤΗ ΤΗΣ ΚΑΤΣΑΡΟΛΑΣ κότα ψητή της κατσαρόλας kota psiti tis katsarolas *roast chicken*

beer
bira

beef
mosKHari

chicken
kotopoolo

lamb
arni

ΛΑΧΑΝΟΝΤΟΛΜΑΔΕΣ λαχανοντολμάδες laκΗanodolmathes *cabbage leaves stuffed with rice and mince*

ΜΑΚΑΡΟΝΙΑ ΜΕ ΚΙΜΑ μακαρόνια με κιμά makaronia meh kima *spaghetti bolognaise*

ΜΟΥΣΑΚΑΣ μουσακάς moosakas *moussaka, layers of either aubergine or potatoes and minced meat topped with thick creamy sauce and baked*

ΜΟΣΧΑΡΙ ΚΟΚΚΙΝΙΣΤΟ μοσχάρι κοκκινιστό mosκΗari kokinisto *veal in tomato sauce*

ΠΑΣΤΙΤΣΙΟ παστίτσιο pastitsio *macaroni, minced meat and thick creamy sauce*

ΠΙΠΕΡΙΕΣ ΓΕΜΙΣΤΕΣ πιπεριές γεμιστές piperi-es yemistes *stuffed green peppers*

ΣΤΙΦΑΔΟ στιφάδο stifatho *hare or rabbit stew with onions*

ΓΙΟΥΒΑΡΛΑΚΙΑ γιουβαρλάκια yoovarlakia *minced meat, rice and seasoning in sauce*

ΓΙΟΥΒΕΤΣΙ γιουβέτσι yoovetsi *roast lamb with pasta*

ΘΑΛΑΣΣΙΝΑ THalasina *seafood*

ΑΣΤΑΚΟΣ αστακός astakos *lobster*

ΜΠΑΚΑΛΙΑΡΟΣ μπακαλιάρος bakaliaros *cod*

ΓΑΡΙΔΕΣ γαρίδες garithes *prawns*

ΚΑΛΑΜΑΡΑΚΙΑ καλαμαράκια kalamarakia *fried baby squid*

ΚΑΒΟΥΡΙΑ καβούρια kavooria *boiled crab*

ΜΥΔΙΑ μύδια mithia *mussels*

ΤΥΡΙΑ tirya *cheeses*

ΑΝΘΟΤΥΡΟ ανθότυρο anTHotiro *aromatic cheese*

ΦΕΤΑ φέτα feta *soft white cheese*

ΚΑΣΕΡΙ κασέρι kaseri *mild yellow cheese*

ΚΕΦΑΛΟΤΥΡΙ κεφαλοτύρι kefalotiri *hard cheese, very salty*

ΜΑΝΟΥΡΙ μανούρι manoori *hard cheese*

ΓΛΥΚΑ glika *sweets*

ΑΜΥΓΔΑΛΩΤΑ αμυγδαλωτά amigthalota *almond pastries*

ΜΠΑΚΛΑΒΑΣ μπακλαβάς baklavas *pastry filled with nuts and syrup*

ΓΑΛΑΚΤΟΜΠΟΥΡΕΚΟ γαλακτομπούρεκο galaktobooreko *thin pastry with custard filling*

ΚΑΤΑΪΦΙ καταΐφι kata-ifi *shredded pastry with nuts and honey*

ΚΟΥΡΑΜΠΙΕΔΕΣ κουραμπιέδες koorabi-ethes *Greek shortbread*

ΛΟΥΚΟΥΜΑΔΕΣ λουκουμάδες lookoomathes *fritters coated in honey*

ΜΕΛΟΜΑΚΑΡΟΝΑ μελομακάρονα melomakarona *fritters coated in nuts and syrup*

ΠΑΓΩΤΟ παγωτό pagoto *ice cream*

ΠΟΡΤΟΚΑΛΙ πορτοκάλι portokali *orange, boiled and sugared*

ΒΑΝΙΛΙΑ βανίλια vanilia *hard vanilla-flavoured sweet, served in a glass of water with a spoon*

ΒΥΣΣΙΝΟ βύσσινο visino *cherries, boiled and sugared*

coffee
kafes

vanilla
vanilia

strawberry
fraoola

chocolate
sokolata

the bill, please
ton logariasmo, parakalo

metre to metro [το μέτρο]

✈ 1 metre = 39.37 inches = 1.09 yds

metro o ipoyios [ο υπόγειος]
midday to mesimeri [το μεσημέρι]
at midday to mesimeri [το μεσημέρι]
middle to meso [το μέσο]
in the middle sti mesi [στη μέση]
midnight ta mesanikta [τα μεσάνυκτα]
might: he might have gone *bori* na eKHi fiyi [μπορεί να έχει φύγει]
migraine i imikrania [η ημικρανία]
mild ipios [ήπιος]
mile ena mili [ένα μίλι]

✈ miles/5 x 8 = kilometres

miles	0.5	1	3	5	10	50	100
kilometres	0.8	1.6	4.8	8	16	80	160

milk to gala [το γάλα]
a glass of milk ena potiri gala [ένα ποτήρι γάλα]
milkshake ena 'milkshake' [ένα μιλκσέικ]
millimetre ena KHiliosto [ένα χιλιοστό]
milometer o KHiliometritis [ο χιλιομετρητής]
minaret enas minares [ένας μιναρές]
mind: I've changed my mind alaksa gnomi [άλλαξα γνώμη]
I don't mind then meh pirazi [δεν με πειράζει]
do you mind if I...? THa seh pirazeh an...? [θα σε πείραζε αν...;]
never mind then pirazi [δεν πειράζει]
mine thikos moo [δικός μου]
mineral water ena metaliko nero [ένα μεταλλικό νερό]
minimum elaKHistos [ελάχιστος]
minus plin [πλην]

minute to lepto [το λεπτό]
in a minute seh ena lepto [σε ένα λεπτό]
just a minute ena lepto [ένα λεπτό]
mirror o kaTHreftis [ο καθρέφτης]
Miss thespinis [Δις]
miss: I miss you moo lipis [μου λείπεις]
he's missing lipi [λείπει]
there is a... missing lipi ena... [λείπει ένα...]
we missed the bus KHasameh to leoforio [χάσαμε το λεωφορείο]
mist i omiKHli [η ομίχλη]
mistake ena laTHos [ένα λάθος]
I think you've made a mistake nomizo oti eKHeteh kani laTHos [νομίζω ότι έχετε κάνει λάθος]
misunderstanding mia pareksiyisi [μιά παρεξήγηση]
mobile (phone) ena kinito (tilefono) [ένα κινητό (τηλέφωνο)]
my mobile number is... o ariTHmos too kinitoo moo ineh... [ο αριθμός του κινητού μου είναι...]
modern modernos [μοντέρνος]
moisturizer mia ithatiki krema [μιά υδατική κρέμα]
Monday theftera [Δευτέρα]
money ta lefta [τα λεφτά]
I've lost my money eKHasa ta lefta moo [έχασα τα λεφτά μου]
I have no money then eKHo kaTHoloo lefta [δεν έχω καθόλου λεφτά]
money belt mia banana [μιά μπανάνα]
month o minas [ο μήνας]
moon to fengari [το φεγγάρι]
moorings i primatses [οι πρυμάτσες]
moped ena miKHanaki [ένα μηχανάκι]

more perisotero [περισσότερο]
can I have some more? boro na eкнo akomi ligo? [μπορώ να έχω ακόμη λίγο;]
more wine, please ki *alo* krasi, parakalo [κι άλλο κρασί, παρακαλώ]
no more thanks ftani, efкнaristo [φτάνει, ευχαριστώ]
more than that perisotero apo afto [περισσότερο από αυτό]
more comfortable pio anapaftiki [πιό αναπαυτική]
morning to pro-i [το πρωί]
good morning kalimera [καλημέρα]
in the morning to pro-i [το πρωί]
this morning simera to pro-i [σήμερα το πρωί]
mosque to tzami [το τζαμί]
mosquito ena koonoopi [ένα κουνούπι]
most: I like this one the most moo aresi afto pio poli apo ola [μου αρέσει αυτό πιό πολύ από όλα]
most of the people i perisoteri anтнropi [οι περισσότεροι άνθρωποι]
mother: my mother i mitera moo [η μητέρα μου]
motor i mikнani [η μηχανή]
motorbike ena motosako [ένα μοτοσακό]
motorboat mia venzinakatos [μιά βενζινάκατος]
motorcyclist o motosikletistis [ο μοτοσυκλετιστής]
(female) i motosikletistria [η μοτοσυκλετίστρια]
motorist o/i othigos aftokinitoo [ο/η οδηγός αυτοκινήτου]
motorway i eтнniki othos [η εθνική οδός]
mountain to voono [το βουνό]
mouse *(also for computer)* ena pondiki [ένα ποντίκι]
moustache to moostaki [το μουστάκι]
mouth to stoma [το στόμα]
move: don't move stop [στοπ]
could you move your car? boriteh na

metakiniseteh to aftokinito sas? [μπορείτε να μετακινήσετε το αυτοκίνητό σας;]
movie i tenia [η ταινία]
MPV ena epsilon omikron [ένα Ε.Ο.]
Mr kirios [Κος]
Mrs kiria [Κα]
Ms *no equivalent*
much poli [πολύ]
much better poli kalitera [πολύ καλύτερα]
not much oKHi poli [όχι πολύ]
mug: I've been mugged meh listepsan [με λήστεψαν]
mum: my mum i mama moo [η μαμά μου]
muscle o mis [ο μυς]
museum to moosio [το μουσείο]

✈ You normally pay to go into Greek museums except on Sundays and public holidays.

mushrooms ta manitaria [τα μανιτάρια]
music i moosiki [η μουσική]
must: I must... prepi na... [πρέπει να...]
I must not eat... then prepi na fao... [δεν πρέπει να φάω...]
must I...? prepi na...? [πρέπει να...;]
you mustn't... then prepi na... [δεν πρέπει να...]
mustard i moostartha [η μουστάρδα]
my

To say 'my...' you wrap the Greek for 'the' (either of **o**/**i**/**to**) and the word **moo** around what is mine.
my hotel to ksenothoKHio moo [το ξενοδοχείο μου]

N

nail *(on finger)* to nikHi [το νύχι]
(for wood) ena karfi [ένα καρφί]
nail clippers enas onikHokoptis [ένας ονυχοκόπτης]
nail file mia lima nikHion [μιά λίμα νυχιών]
nail polish ena mano [ένα μανό]
nail scissors ena psalithi ya nikHia [ένα ψαλίδι για νύχια]
naked yimnos [γυμνός]
name to onoma [το όνομα]
my name is... meh leneh... [με λένε...]
what's your name? pos seh leneh? [πώς σε λένε;]
napkin mia petseta [μιά πετσέτα]
nappy mia pana [μιά πάνα]
narrow stenos [στενός]
national eTHnikos [εθνικός]
nationality i eTHnikotita [η εθνικότητα]
natural fisikos [φυσικός]
naughty: don't be naughty *(to man/woman)* min iseh ataktos/atakti [μην είσαι άτακτος/άτακτη]
near: is it near? ineh konda? [είναι κοντά;]
near here etho konda [εδώ κοντά]
do you go near...? pas konda sto...? [πας κοντά στο...;]
where's the nearest...? poo ineh to plisi-estero...? [πού είναι το πλησιέστερο...;]
nearly sKHethon [σχεδόν]
neat *(drink)* sketos [σκέτος]
necessary anangeos [αναγκαίος]
it's not necessary then KHriazeteh [δεν χρειάζεται]
neck o lemos [ο λαιμός]
necklace to koli-eh [το κολλιέ]
need: I need a... KHriazomeh ena... [χρειάζομαι

ένα...]
needle mia velona [μιά βελόνα]
neighbour o yitonas [ο γείτονας]
(female) i yitonisa [η γειτόνισσα]
neither: neither of them kanenas apo toos thio [κανένας από τους δύο]
neither... nor ooteh... ooteh [ούτε... ούτε]
neither do I ooteh ki ego [ούτε κι εγώ]
neither am I ooteh ki ego [ούτε κι εγώ]
nephew: my nephew o anipsios moo [ο ανηψιός μου]
nervous taragmenos [ταραγμένος]
net *(fishing)* to thiKHti [το δίχτυ]
never poteh [ποτέ]
new neos [νέος]
(not used) kenooryos [καινούριος]
news ta nea [τα νέα]
newsagent's ena praktorio efimerithon [ένα πρακτορείο εφημερίδων]
newspaper mia efimeritha [μιά εφημερίδα]
do you have any English newspapers? eKHeteh anglikes efimerithes? [έχετε Αγγλικές εφημερίδες;]
New Year to neo etos [το Νέο Έτος]
Happy New Year KHaroomeni protoKHronia [Χαρούμενη Πρωτοχρονιά]

✈ All lights are briefly switched off for midnight; after midnight it's a Greek custom to play cards.

New Year's Eve paramoni protoKHronias [Παραμονή Πρωτοχρονιάς]
New Zealand i nea zilanthia [η Νέα Ζηλανδία]
next epomenos [επόμενος]
please stop at the next corner parakalo, stamatisteh stin epomeni strofi [παρακαλώ, σταματήστε στην επόμενη στροφή]

see you next year THa seh tho too KHronoo [θα σε δω του χρόνου]
next week tin ali evthomatha [την άλλη εβδομάδα]
next Tuesday tin ali triti [την άλλη Τρίτη]
next to the hotel *thipla* sto ksenothoKHio [δίπλα στο ξενοδοχείο]
next of kin o pio stenos singenis [ο πιό στενός συγγενής]
nice oreos [ωραίος]
(person) kalos [καλός]
(pleasant, kind) evgenikos [ευγενικός]
niece: my niece i anipsia moo [η ανηψιά μου]
night to vrathi [το βράδυ]
good night kaliniKHta [καληνύχτα]
at night to vrathi [το βράδυ]
night club ena 'nightclub' [ένα 'night club']
nightdress ena niKHtiko [ένα νυχτικό]
night porter o niKHterinos THiroros [ο νυχτερινός θυρωρός]
no oKHi [όχι]
there's no water then eKHi nero [δεν έχει νερό]
I have no... then eKHo... [δεν έχω...]
no way! apokli-eteh! [αποκλείεται!]

✈ Rolling the head upwards and back means 'no' in Greece.

nobody kanenas [κανένας]
nobody saw it kanenas then to itheh [κανένας δεν το είδε]
noisy THorivothis [θορυβώδης]
our room is too noisy to thomatio mas eKHi poli fasaria [το δωμάτιό μας έχει πολύ φασαρία]
none kanenas [κανένας]
none of them kanenas apo aftoos [κανένας από αυτούς]
non-smoker: we're non-smokers then

kapnizoomeh [δεν καπνίζουμε]
normal fisioloyikos [φυσιολογικός]
north o voras [ο βορράς]
Northern Ireland i vorios irlanthia [η Βόρειος Ιρλανδία]
nose i miti [η μύτη]
not *(with verbs)* then [δεν]
  not that one oKHi afto [όχι αυτό]
  not me oKHi ego [όχι εγώ]
  I'm not hungry then pinao [δεν πεινάω]
  he didn't tell me then moo to ipeh [δεν μου το είπε]
note *(bank note)* to KHartonomisma [το χαρτονόμισμα]
nothing tipota [τίποτα]
November noemvrios [Νοέμβριος]
now tora [τώρα]
nowhere pooTHena [πουθενά]
nudist beach mia paralia yimniston [μιά παραλία γυμνιστών]
nuisance: it's a nuisance ineh belas [είναι μπελάς]
  this man's being a nuisance aftos o andras ineh enoKHlitikos [αυτός ο άνδρας είναι ενοχλητικός]
numb moothiasmenos [μουδιασμένος]
number *(figure)* o ariTHmos [ο αριθμός]
number plate i pinakithes [οι πινακίδες]
nurse mia nosokoma [μιά νοσοκόμα]
  (male) enas nosokomos [ένας νοσοκόμος]
nut to karithi [το καρύδι]
  (for bolt) ena paximathi [ένα παξιμάδι]

oar to koopi [το κουπί]
obligatory ipoKHreotikos [υποχρεωτικός]
obviously profanos [προφανώς]
occasionally kamia fora [καμιά φορά]

o'clock *go to* **time**
October oktovrios [Οκτώβριος]
octopus ena KHtapothi [ένα χταπόδι]
odd *(number)* monos [μονός]
(strange) paraksenos [παράξενος]
of too [του]
the name of the hotel to onoma too ksenothoKHioo [το όνομα του ξενοδοχείου]
off: the milk is off to gala KHalaseh [το γάλα χάλασε]
it just came off v-yikeh apo mono too [βγήκε από μόνο του]
10% off theka tis ekato ekptosi [10% έκπτωση]
office to grafio [το γραφείο]
officer *(to policeman)* kiri-eh astinomeh [κύριε αστυνόμε]
(to policewoman) kiria astinomeh [κυρία αστυνόμε]
official enas anoteros ipalilos [ένας ανώτερος υπάλληλος]
often siKHna [συχνά]
not often oKHi siKHna [όχι συχνά]
how often? poso siKHna? [πόσο συχνά;]
how often do the buses go? poso siKHna piyenoon ta leoforia? [πόσο συχνά πηγαίνουν τα λεωφορεία;]

YOU MAY THEN HEAR
kaTHeh theka lepta *every ten minutes*
thio fores tin imera *twice a day*

oil to lathi [το λάδι]
will you change the oil? boriteh na moo alakseteh ta lathia? [μπορείτε να μου αλλάξετε τα λάδια;]
ointment mia alifi [μιά αλοιφή]
ok endaksi [εντάξει]
it's ok *(doesn't matter)* then pirazi [δεν πειράζει]
are you ok? iseh kala? [είσαι καλά;]

that's ok by me then eKHo andirisi [δεν έχω αντίρρηση]
is this ok for the airport? piyeni sto a-erothromio? [πηγαίνει στο αεροδρόμιο;]
more wine? – no, I'm ok thanks THelis alo krasi? – oKHi, efKHaristo, imeh endaksi [θέλεις άλλο κρασί; όχι, ευχαριστώ, είμαι εντάξει]
old *(person)* yeros [γέρος]
(thing) palios [παλιός]
how old are you? poso KHronon iseh? [πόσο χρονών είσαι;]

I'm 28 imeh ikosi oKHto KHronon [είμαι 28 χρονών]

olive i elia [η ελιά]
olive oil to eleolatho [το ελαιόλαδο]
omelette mia omeleta [μιά ομελέτα]
on pano [πάνω]
on the bar pano sto bar [πάνω στο μπαρ]
I haven't got it on me then to eKHo mazi moo [δεν το έχω μαζί μου]
on Friday tin paraskevi [την Παρασκευή]
on television stin tileorasi [στην τηλεόραση]
once mia fora [μιά φορά]
at once *(immediately)* amesos [αμέσως]
one enas/mia/ena [ένας/μία/ένα]
(number) ena [ένα]
the red one to kokino [το κόκκινο]
onion ena kremithi [ένα κρεμμύδι]
on-line: to pay on-line plirono meso thiathiktioo [πληρώνω μέσω διαδικτύου]
only mono [μόνο]
the only one to mono [το μόνο]
open *(adjective)* aniktos [ανοικτός]
I can't open it then boro na to anikso [δεν μπορώ να το ανοίξω]
when do you open? poteh aniyeteh?

[πότε ανοίγετε;]
open ticket ena isitirio meh anikti epistrofi [ένα εισιτήριο με ανοικτή επιστροφή]
opera i opera [η όπερα]
operation mia enKHirisi [μιά εγχείρηση]
operator *(telephone)* o tilefonitis too kendroo [ο τηλεφωνητής του κέντρου]

✈ The international operator is on 161.

opposite: opposite the hotel apenandi apo to ksenothoKHio [απέναντι από το ξενοδοχείο]
optician's ena katastima optikon ithon [ένα κατάστημα οπτικών ειδών]
or i [ή]
orange *(fruit)* ena portokali [ένα πορτοκάλι]
(colour) portokali [πορτοκαλί]
orange juice enas KHimos portokalioo [ένας χυμός πορτοκαλιού]
order: could we order now? boroomeh na parangiloomeh tora? [μπορούμε να παραγγείλουμε τώρα;]
thank you, we've already ordered efKHaristo, eKHoomeh ithi parangili [ευχαριστώ, έχουμε ήδη παραγγείλει]
other: the other one to alo [το άλλο]
do you have any others? eKHeteh tipota ala? [έχετε τίποτα άλλα;]
otherwise thiaforetika [διαφορετικά]
ought: I ought to go prepi na figo [πρέπει να φύγω]
our

To say 'our...' you wrap the Greek for 'the' (either of **o**/**i**/**to**) and the word **mas** around what is ours.
our hotel to ksenothoKHio mas [το ξενοδοχείο μας]

ours thikos mas [δικός μας]
out: we're out of petrol minameh apo venzini [μείναμε από βενζίνη]
get out! v-yes ekso! [βγες έξω!]
outboard i eksolemvios [η εξωλέμβιος]
outdoors ekso [έξω]
outside: can we sit outside? boroomeh na kaTHisoomeh ekso? [μπορούμε να καθήσουμε έξω;]
over: over here etho [εδώ]
over there eki [εκεί]
over 40 pano apo 40 [πάνω από 40]
it's all over *(finished)* ola teliosan [όλα τελείωσαν]
overcharge: you've overcharged me meh KHreosateh parapano [με χρεώσατε παραπάνω]
overcooked parapsimenos [παραψημένος]
overexposed para-ekteTHimenos [παραεκτεθειμένος]
overnight ti niKHta [τη νύχτα]
oversleep: I overslept parakimiTHika [παρακοιμήθηκα]
overtake prosperno [προσπερνώ]
owe: what do I owe you? poso sas ofilo? [πόσο σας οφείλω;]
own: my own... o thikos moo... [ο δικός μου...]
I'm on my own imeh monos/moni moo [είμαι μόνος/μόνη μου]
owner o ithioktitis [ο ιδιοκτήτης]
(female) i ithioktitria [η ιδιοκτήτρια]
oxygen to oksigono [το οξυγόνο]
oysters ta strithia [τα στρείδια]

P

pack: I haven't packed yet then *ekana tis valitses* moo akoma [δεν έκανα τις βαλίτσες μου ακόμα]

can I have a packed lunch? boroomeh na paroomeh paketarismeno fayito? [μπορούμε να πάρουμε πακεταρισμένο φαγητό;]
package tour mia organomeni ekthromi [μιά οργανωμένη εκδρομή]
page *(of book)* i selitha [η σελίδα]
could you page him? boriteh na ton ithopi-iseteh? [μπορείτε να τον ειδοποιήσετε;]
pain o ponos [ο πόνος]
I've got a pain in my... eKHo enan pono sto... moo [έχω έναν πόνο στο... μου]
pain-killers ta pafsipona [τα παυσίπονα]
painting *(picture)* o pinakas [ο πίνακας]
Pakistan to pakistan [το Πακιστάν]
pale KHlomos [χλωμός]
pancake mia tiganita [μιά τηγανίτα]
panties i kilotes [οι κυλότες]
pants ta pantalonia [τα παντελόνια]
(underpants) to slipaki [το σλιπάκι]
paper to KHarti [το χαρτί]
(newspaper) mia efimeritha [μιά εφημερίδα]
parcel ena paketo [ένα πακέτο]
pardon? *(didn't understand)* signomi? [συγγνώμη;]
I beg your pardon *(sorry)* meh sinKHoriteh [με συγχωρείτε]
parents: my parents i gonis moo [οι γονείς μου]
park to parko [το πάρκο]
where can I park my car? poo boro na parkaro to aftokinito moo? [πού μπορώ να παρκάρω το αυτοκίνητό μου;]
is it difficult to get parked? ineh thiskolo na vro KHoro ya parkarisma? [είναι δύσκολο να βρω χώρο για παρκάρισμα;]
parking ticket mia klisi ya paranomo parkarisma [μιά κλήση για παράνομο παρκάρισμα]
part ena meros [ένα μέρος]
a (spare) part ena andalaktiko

[ένα ανταλλακτικό]

partner *(boyfriend, girlfriend etc)* o/i sindrofos [ο/η σύντροφος]

party *(group)* i omatha [η ομάδα]
(celebration) ena parti [ένα πάρτυ]
I'm with the...party imeh meh tin...omatha [είμαι με την...ομάδα]

pass *(in mountain)* ena perasma [ένα πέρασμα]
he's passed out lipoTHimiseh [λιποθύμησε]

passable *(road)* thiavatos [διαβατός]

passenger o/i epivatis [ο/η επιβάτης]

passer-by o/i thiavatis [ο/η διαβάτης]

passport to thiavatirio [το διαβατήριο]

past: in the past sto parelTHon [στο παρελθόν]
it's just past the traffic lights ineh amesos *meta* ta fanaria [είναι αμέσως μετά τα φανάρια]
go to **time**

path to monopati [το μονοπάτι]

patient: be patient kaneh ipomoni [κάνε υπομονή]

pattern ena sKHethio [ένα σχέδιο]

pavement to pezothromio [το πεζοδρόμιο]

pavement café ena kafenio ston thromo [ένα καφενείο στον δρόμο]

pay plirono [πληρώνω]
can I pay, please? boro na pliroso, parakalo? [μπορώ να πληρώσω, παρακαλώ;]

✈ You normally pay when you leave, not when you order your drinks.

peace *(calm)* i iremia [η ηρεμία]
(not war) i irini [η ειρήνη]

peach ena rothakino [ένα ροδάκινο]

peanuts ta fistikia arapika [τα φυστίκια αράπικα]

pear ena aKHlathi [ένα αχλάδι]

peas ta bizelia [τα μπιζέλια]

pedal to petali [το πετάλι]

pedestrian o pezos [ο πεζός]
(woman) i pezi [η πεζή]
pedestrian crossing mia thiavasi pezon [μιά διάβαση πεζών]

> ✈ Don't assume that cars will always stop for you!

peg *(for washing)* ena mandalaki [ένα μανταλάκι]
(for tent) ena palooki [ένα παλούκι]
pen ena stilo [ένα στυλό]
have you got a pen? eKHeteh ena stilo [έχετε ένα στυλό;]
pencil ena molivi [ένα μολύβι]
penicillin i penikilini [η πενικιλλίνη]
penknife enas sooyas [ένας σουγιάς]
pensioner enas/mia sindaksiooKHos [ένας/μιά συνταξιούχος]
people i anTHropi [οι άνθρωποι]
how many people? posa atoma? [πόσα άτομα;]
people carrier ena epivatiko oKHima [ένα επιβατικό όχημα]
pepper to piperi [το πιπέρι]
green/red pepper mia prasini/kokini piperia [μιά πράσινη/κόκκινη πιπεριά]
peppermint mia menta [μιά μέντα]
per: per night/week/person to vrathi/tin evthomatha/to atomo [το βράδυ/την εβδομάδα/το άτομο]
per cent tis ekato [τοις εκατό]
perfect telios [τέλειος]
perfume ena aroma [ένα άρωμα]
perhaps isos [ίσως]
period *(of time, woman)* mia periothos [μιά περίοδος]
permit mia athia [μιά άδεια]
person ena atomo [ένα άτομο]
in person prosopika [προσωπικά]

personal stereo ena 'walkman'® [ένα 'walkman']
petrol i venzini [η βενζίνη]
petrol station ena venzinathiko [ένα βενζινάδικο]

> ✈ Either 3-star **apli** (regular), 4-star (**sooper**) or unleaded (**amolivthi**). Most petrol stations are staffed, not self-service; *go to* **garage**.

pharmacy to farmakio [το φαρμακείο]

> ✈ They'll help with minor medical complaints.

phone to tilefono [το τηλέφωνο]
I'll phone you THa soo tilefoniso [θα σου τηλεφωνήσω]
I'll phone you back THa seh paro piso argotera [θα σε πάρω πίσω αργότερα]
can you phone back in five minutes? boris na meh paris piso seh pendeh lepta? [μπορείς να με πάρεις πίσω σε πέντε λεπτά;]

can I speak to Maria? boro na miliso sti maria? [μπορώ να μιλήσω στη Μαρία;]
could you get the number for me? boriteh na moo pareteh ton ariTHmo? [μπορείτε να μου πάρετε τον αριθμό;]

YOU MAY HEAR
o sinthromitis poo kalesateh then apanda *the number you have called is not answering*
parakalo kalesteh argotera *please call later*
o sinthromitis poo kalesateh then iparKHi *the number you have called has not been recognized*

> ✈ **OTE** (Greek Telecom) offices open from 7 am to 10 or 11 pm (or sometimes stay open 24 hours in major cities). You can also

make calls, though it might cost you more, from newspaper and tobacco kiosks, which is where you can also buy phonecards. You'll need a phonecard for any public phone in Athens. The code for the UK is 0044, dropping the first 0 of the UK area code.

phonebox enas tilefonikos THalamos [ένας τηλεφωνικός θάλαμος]
phonecall to tilefonima [το τηλεφώνημα]
can I make a phonecall? boro na tilefoniso? [μπορώ να τηλεφωνήσω;]
phonecard mia tilekarta [μιά τηλεκάρτα]
photograph mia fotografia [μιά φωτογραφία]
would you take a photograph of us/me? boriteh na mas/moo vgaleteh mia fotografia? [μπορείτε να μας/μου βγάλετε μιά φωτογραφία;]
piano ena piano [ένα πιάνο]
pickpocket enas portofolas [ένας πορτοφολάς]
picture mia ikona [μιά εικόνα]
piece ena komati [ένα κομμάτι]
a piece of... ena komati apo... [ένα κομμάτι από...]
pig ena goorooni [ένα γουρούνι]
pigeon ena peristeri [ένα περιστέρι]
pile-up mia karabola [μιά καραμπόλα]
pill to KHapi [το χάπι]
are you on the pill? pernis to KHapi? [παίρνεις το χάπι;]
pillow ena maksilari [ένα μαξιλάρι]
pin mia karfitsa [μιά καρφίτσα]
pineapple enas ananas [ένας ανανάς]
pink roz [ροζ]
pint mia pinda [μιά πίντα]

✈ 1 pint = 0.57 litres

pipe *(to smoke)* mia pipa [μιά πίπα]
(for water) o solinas [ο σωλήνας]
pistachios ta fistikia eyinis [τα φυστίκια Αιγίνης]
pitta bread mia pita [μιά πίττα]
pity: it's a pity ineh krima [είναι κρίμα]
place ena meros [ένα μέρος]
is this place taken? ineh piasmeni afti i THesi? [είναι πιασμένη αυτή η θέση;]
do you know any good places to go? ksereteh tipota kala meri na pao? [ξέρετε τίποτα καλά μέρη να πάω;]
at my place sto spiti moo [στο σπίτι μου]
at your place sto spiti soo [στο σπίτι σου]
to your place sto spiti soo [στο σπίτι σου]
plain sketos [σκέτος]
a plain omelette mia sketi omeleta [μιά σκέτη ομελέτα]
plane to aeroplano [το αεροπλάνο]
plant to fito [το φυτό]
plaster *(cast)* o yipsos [ο γύψος]
(sticking) ena lefkoplast [ένα λευκοπλάστ]
plastic plastikos [πλαστικός]
plastic bag mia nailon sakoola [μιά νάυλον σακούλα]
plate ena piato [ένα πιάτο]
platform mia platforma [μιά πλατφόρμα]
which platform please? pia platforma, parakalo? [ποιά πλατφόρμα, παρακαλώ;]
play *(verb)* pezo [παίζω]
pleasant efkHaristos [ευχάριστος]
please: could you please...? parakalo, boriteh...? [παρακαλώ, μπορείτε...;]
(yes) please neh, parakalo [ναι, παρακαλώ]
pleasure i efkHaristisi [η ευχαρίστηση]
it's a pleasure KHara moo [χαρά μου]
plenty: plenty of... pola... [πολλά...]
thank you, that's plenty efkHaristo, afto ineh

arketo [ευχαριστώ, αυτό είναι αρκετό]
pliers mia pensa [μιά πένσα]
plug *(electrical)* i priza [η πρίζα]
(for car) to boozi [το μπουζί]
(for sink) mia tapa [μιά τάπα]

✈ *go to* **electricity**

plum ena thamaskino [ένα δαμάσκηνο]
plumber enas ithravlikos [ένας υδραυλικός]
plus sin [συν]
pm m.m., meta mesimvrias [μ.μ., μετά μεσημβρίας]
pocket i tsepi [η τσέπη]
point: could you point to it? boriteh na to thikseteh? [μπορείτε να το δείξετε;]
4 point 6 tesera *koma* eksi [τέσσερα κόμμα έξι]
police i astinomia [η αστυνομία]
get the police ithopi-isteh tin astinomia [ειδοποιήστε την αστυνομία]

✈ Dial 100 for the police and 171 for the Tourist Police (**tooristiki astinomia**).

policeman o astinomikos [ο αστυνομικός]
police station to astinomiko tmima [το αστυνομικό τμήμα]
policewoman i astinomikos [η αστυνομικός]
polish to verniki [το βερνίκι]
can you polish my shoes? boriteh na moo yaliseteh ta papootsia? [μπορείτε να μου γυαλίσετε τα παπούτσια;]
polite evyenikos [ευγενικός]
polluted molismenos [μολυσμένος]
pool *(swimming)* i pisina [η πισίνα]
poor: I'm very poor imeh poli ftoKHos/ftoKHi [είμαι πολύ φτωχός/φτωχή]
poor quality kaki piotita [κακή ποιότητα]
pork to KHirino [το χοιρινό]

port to limani [το λιμάνι]
(drink) ena port [ένα πορτ]
(not starboard) aristeri plevra plioo [αριστερή πλευρά πλοίου]
porter o aKHTHoforos [ο αχθοφόρος]
portrait ena portreto [ένα πορτραίτο]
Portugal i portogalia [η Πορτογαλία]
posh *(hotel etc)* politelis [πολυτελής]
(people) kirilethes [κυριλέδες]
possible piTHanos [πιθανός]
could you possibly...? THa sas itan thinato na...? [θα σας ήταν δυνατό να...;]
post *(mail)* ta gramata [τα γράμματα]
postbox ena gramatokivotio [ένα γραμματοκιβώτιο]
postcard mia karta [μιά κάρτα]
poste restante post-restant [ποστ-ρεστάντ]
post office to taKHithromio [το ταχυδρομείο]

✈ Open 8 am to 2.30 pm Mon-Fri. Avoid buying stamps in places other than the post office.

potatoes i patates [οι πατάτες]
pound i livra [η λίβρα]
(money) i lira anglias [η λίρα Αγγλίας]

✈ pounds/11 x 5 = kilos

pounds	1	3	5	6	7	8	9
kilos	0.45	1.4	2.3	2.7	3.2	3.6	4.1

pour: it's pouring vreKHi kataraktothos [βρέχει καταρρακτωδώς]
power cut mia thiakopi revmatos [μιά διακοπή ρεύματος]
power point i priza [η πρίζα]
prawns i garithes [οι γαρίδες]
prefer: I prefer this one protimo afto [προτιμώ αυτό]

I'd prefer to... THa protimoosa na... [θα προτιμούσα να...]
I'd prefer a... THa protimoosa ena... [θα προτιμούσα ένα...]
pregnant engios [έγκυος]
prescription mia sintayi [μιά συνταγή]
present: at present pros to paron [προς το παρόν]
here's a present for you afto ineh ena *thoro* ya sena [αυτό είναι ένα δώρο για σένα]
president *(of country)* o/i proethros [ο/η πρόεδρος]
press: could you press these? boriteh na sitheroseteh afta? [μπορείτε να σιδερώσετε αυτά;]
pretty oreos [ωραίος]
pretty good poli kalo [πολύ καλό]
price i timi [η τιμή]
priest o papas [ο παπάς]
prison i filaki [η φυλακή]
private ithiotikos [ιδιωτικός]
probably piTHanos [πιθανώς]
problem ena provlima [ένα πρόβλημα]
no problem! kanena provlima! [κανένα πρόβλημα!]
product ena pro-ion [ένα προϊόν]
profit to kerthos [το κέρδος]
promise: do you promise? iposkHeseh? [υπόσχεσαι;]
I promise iposkHomeh [υπόσχομαι]
pronounce: how do you pronounce this? pos profereteh afto? [πώς προφέρεται αυτό;]
propeller i propela [η προπέλλα]
properly opos prepi [όπως πρέπει]
prostitute mia porni [μιά πόρνη]
protect prostatevo [προστατεύω]
protection factor o vaTHmos prostasias [ο βαθμός προστασίας]

Protestant protestandis [Προτεστάντης]
proud iperifanos [υπερήφανος]
public: the public to kino [το κοινό]
public convenience mia thimosia tooaleta [μιά δημόσια τουαλέτα]

✈ Few and far between; *more at* **toilet**.

public holiday mia thimosia aryia [μιά δημόσια αργία]

✈ Greek public holidays:

New Year's Day i protoкнronia [η Πρωτοχρονιά]
Epiphany (6 January) ta тнeofania [τα Θεοφάνεια]
KaтнarA Deftera (its date each year depends on when Easter falls) [η Καθαρά Δευτέρα]
25th of March i ikosti pempti martioo [η εικοστή πέμπτη Μαρτίου]
Easter to paskнa [το Πάσχα]
1st of May i protomaya [η Πρωτομαγιά]
8th of June too a-yioo pnevmatos [του Αγίου Πνεύματος]
15th of August o thekapendavgoostos [ο Δεκαπενταύγουστος]
28th of October i ikosti ogtho-i oktovrioo [η εικοστή ογδόη Οκτωβρίου]
Christmas Day ta кнristooyena [τα Χριστούγεννα]

pudding mia pootinga [μιά πουτίγκα]
pull *(verb)* travo [τραβώ]
he pulled out in front of me estripseh keh ilтнeh brosta moo [έστριψε και ήλθε μπροστά μου]
pump i andlia [η αντλία]
puncture mia tripa sto lastiкнo [μιά τρύπα στο λάστιχο]

pure agnos [αγνός]
purple mov [μωβ]
purse to portofoli [το πορτοφόλι]
push *(verb)* sprokнno [σπρώχνω]
pushchair ena karotsaki [ένα καροτσάκι]
put: where can I put...? poo boro na valo...? [πού μπορώ να βάλω...;]
pyjamas i pitzames [οι πυτζάμες]

Q

quality i piotita [η ποιότητα]
quarantine i karandina [η καραντίνα]
quarter ena tetarto [ένα τέταρτο]
a quarter of an hour ena tetarto tis oras [ένα τέταρτο της ώρας]
go to **time**
quay i provlita [η προβλήτα]
question mia erotisi [μιά ερώτηση]
queue mia oora [μιά ουρά]

✈ Orderly queuing is not widespread.

quick grigora [γρήγορα]
that was quick afto itan grigoro [αυτό ήταν γρήγορο]
quiet isiкнos [ήσυχος]
be quiet! siopi! [σιωπή!]
quite endelos [εντελώς]
(fairly) arketa [αρκετά]
quite a lot para poli [πάρα πολύ]

R

radiator *(of car)* to psiyio aftokinitoo [το ψυγείο αυτοκινήτου]
(in room) to kalorifer [το καλοριφέρ]
radio to rathiofono [το ραδιόφωνο]

rail: by rail sithirothromikos [σιδηροδρομικώς]
rain i vroKHi [η βροχή]
it's raining vreKHi [βρέχει]
raincoat i kapardina [η καπαρντίνα]
rally *(cars)* to rali [το ράλυ]
rape enas viasmos [ένας βιασμός]
rare spanios [σπάνιος]
(steak) oKHi poli psimeno [όχι πολύ ψημένο]
raspberry ena vatomooro [ένα βατόμουρο]
rat enas arooreos [ένας αρουραίος]
rather: I'd rather have a... THa protimoosa ena... [θα προτιμούσα ένα...]
I'd rather not malon oKHi [μάλλον όχι]
raw omos [ωμός]
razor *(dry)* ena ksirafi [ένα ξυράφι]
(electric) mia ksiristiki miKHani [μιά ξυριστική μηχανή]
read: something to read kati na *thiavaso* [κάτι να διαβάσω]
ready: when will it be ready? poteh THa ineh *etimo*? [πότε θα είναι έτοιμο;]
I'm not ready yet then imeh etimos/etimi akomi [δεν είμαι έτοιμος/έτοιμη ακόμη]
real pragmatikos [πραγματικός]
really pragmatika [πραγματικά]
(very) poli [πολύ]
rear-view mirror o kaTHreftis aftokinitoo [ο καθρέφτης αυτοκινήτου]
reasonable lo-yikos [λογικός]
receipt mia apothiksi [μιά απόδειξη]
can I have a receipt please? boriteh na moo thoseteh mia apothiksi, parakalo? [μπορείτε να μου δώσετε μιά απόδειξη, παρακαλώ;]
recently prosfatos [προσφάτως]
reception *(hotel)* i resepsion [η ρεσεψιόν]
in reception sti resepsion [στη ρεσεψιόν]
receptionist o/i resepsionist [ο/η ρεσεψιονίστ]

recipe i sinda-yi [η συνταγή]
recommend: can you recommend...? boriteh na moo sistiseteh...? [μπορείτε να μου συστήσετε...;]
red kokinos [κόκκινος]
reduction *(in price)* mia ekptosi [μιά έκπτωση]
red wine ena kokino krasi [ένα κόκκινο κρασί]
refuse: I refuse arnoomeh [αρνούμαι]
region i periferia [η περιφέρεια]
registered: I want to send this registered THa iTHela na stilo afto *sistimeno* [θα ήθελα να στείλω αυτό συστημένο]
relax: I just want to relax THelo mono na iremiso [θέλω μόνο να ηρεμήσω]
relax! iremiseh! [ηρέμησε!]
remember: don't you remember? then THimaseh? [δεν θυμάσαι;]
I don't remember then THimameh [δεν θυμάμαι]
rent: can I rent a car/bicycle? boro na *nikiaso* ena aftokinito/ena pothilato? [μπορώ να νοικιάσω ένα αυτοκίνητο/ένα ποδήλατο;]

> *YOU MAY HEAR*
> ti marka? *what type?*
> ya poses meres? *for how many days?*
> na to feris piso prin... *bring it back before...*
> mia aperioristi taKHitita seh KHiliometra *unlimited mileage*

rental car ena nikiasmeno aftokinito [ένα νοικιασμένο αυτοκίνητο]
rep o/i andiprosopos [ο/η αντιπρόσωπος]
repair: can you repair it? boriteh na to episkevaseteh? [μπορείτε να το επισκευάσετε;]
repeat: could you repeat that? boriteh na to epanalaveteh? [μπορείτε να το επαναλάβετε;]
reputation i fimi [η φήμη]
rescue *(verb)* sozo [σώζω]

reservation mia kratisi [μιά κράτηση]
I want to make a reservation for... THelo na kratiso THesis ya... [θέλω να κρατήσω θέσεις για...]
reserve: can I reserve a seat? boro na kliso mia THesi? [μπορώ να κλείσω μιά θέση;]

YOU MAY THEN HEAR
ti ora? *for what time?*
ti onoma? *what name is it?*

responsible ipefTHinos [υπεύθυνος]
rest: I've come here for a rest ilTHa etho ya na ksekoorasto [ήλθα εδώ για να ξεκουραστώ]
you keep the rest kratisteh *ta ipolipa* [κρατήστε τα υπόλοιπα]
restaurant ena estiatorio [ένα εστιατόριο]

✈ A **taverna** [ταβέρνα], often in the old town, will be less expensive but probably with a more limited choice (and maybe no menu displayed).

retired sindaksiooKHos [συνταξιούχος]
return: a return to... ena isitirio meh epistrofi sto... [ένα εισιτήριο με επιστροφή στο...]
reverse charge call ena tilefonima kolekt [ένα τηλεφώνημα κολέκτ]
reverse gear i opisTHen [η όπισθεν]
rheumatism i revmatismi [οι ρευματισμοί]
Rhodes i rothos [η Ρόδος]
rib i plevra [η πλευρά]
rice to rizi [το ρύζι]
rich *(person)* ploosios [πλούσιος]
ridiculous yelios [γελοίος]
right: that's right sosta [σωστά]
you're right eKHis thikio [έχεις δίκιο]
on the right sta theksia [στα δεξιά]
right! *(understood)* endaksi! [εντάξει!]

righthand drive othiyisi meh theksio timoni [οδήγηση με δεξιό τιμόνι]
ring *(on finger)* to thaKHtilithi [το δαχτυλίδι]
ripe orimos [ώριμος]
rip-off: it's a rip-off ineh listia [είναι ληστεία]
river to potami [το ποτάμι]
(big) o potamos [ο ποταμός]
road o thromos [ο δρόμος]
which is the road to...? pios ineh o thromos ya...? [ποιός είναι ο δρόμος για...;]
road map enas othikos KHartis [ένας οδικός χάρτης]
rob: I've been robbed meh listepsan [με λήστεψαν]
rock o vraKHos [ο βράχος]
whisky on the rocks ooiski meh pagakia [ουΐσκι με παγάκια]
roll *(bread)* ena psomaki [ένα ψωμάκι]
romantic romandikos [ρομαντικός]
roof i orofi [η οροφή]
roof box to kivotio too aftokinitoo [το κιβώτιο του αυτοκινήτου]
roof rack i sKHara too aftokinitoo [η σχάρα του αυτοκινήτου]
room to thomatio [το δωμάτιο]
have you got a single/double room? eKHeteh ena mono/thiplo thomatio? [έχετε ένα μονό/διπλό δωμάτιο;]

for one night ya mia vrathia [για μία βραδιά]
for three nights ya tris vrathi-es [για τρεις βραδιές]

YOU MAY THEN HEAR
then eKHoomeh *we're full up*
meh banio i KHoris banio? *with or without*

bath?
mono ya...vrathi-es *only for...nights*
to thiavatirio sas parakalo *your passport please*

✈ In smaller towns or villages, information may be obtained from the local tourist office (grafio toorismoo [ΓΡΑΦΕΙΟ ΤΟΥΡΙΣΜΟΥ]). And in smaller towns or villages you might find accommodation in B&Bs or boarding houses (pansion [ΠΑΝΣΙΟΝ]) as well as in hotels.

room service to servis thomatioo [το σέρβις δωματίου]
rope ena sKHini [ένα σχοινί]
rose to triandafilo [το τριαντάφυλλο]
rough *(sea)* trikimiothis [τρικυμιώδης]
roughly *(approx)* pano kato [πάνω κάτω]
round *(circular)* strongilos [στρογγυλός]
it's my round ineh i thiki moo sira na keraso [είναι η δική μου σειρά να κεράσω]
roundabout *(on road)* i thiastavrosi kiklikis kikloforias [η διασταύρωση κυκλικής κυκλοφορίας]

✈ Cars already on a roundabout don't have priority.

route i poria [η πορεία]
which is the prettiest/fastest route? pios ineh o pio oreos/ o pio sindomos thromos? [ποιός είναι ο πιό ωραίος/ο πιό σύντομος δρόμος;]
rowing boat mia varka meh koopia [μιά βάρκα με κουπιά]
rubber *(material)* to lastiKHo [το λάστιχο]
(eraser) mia gomolastiKHa [μιά γομολάστιχα]
rubber band ena lastiKHaki [ένα λαστιχάκι]
rubbish *(waste)* ta skoopithia [τα σκουπίδια]

(poor quality goods) ta skivala [τα σκύβαλα]
rubbish! triKHes! [τρίχες!]
rucksack o sakos [ο σάκος]
rudder to pithalio [το πηδάλιο]
rude ayenis [αγενής]
ruin ena eripio [ένα ερείπιο]
rum ena roomi [ένα ρούμι]
a rum and coke ena roomi meh koka kola [ένα ρούμι με κόκα κόλα]
run: hurry, run! viasoo, *trekseh*! [βιάσου, τρέξε!]
I've run out of petrol/money emina apo venzini/lefta [έμεινα από βενζίνη/λεφτά]

S

sad lipimenos [λυπημένος]
safe asfalis [ασφαλής]
will it be safe here? THa ineh asfales etho? [θα είναι ασφαλές εδώ;]
is it safe to swim here? ineh asfales na kolimbisoomeh etho? [είναι ασφαλές να κολυμπήσουμε εδώ;]
safety i asfalia [η ασφάλεια]
safety pin mia paramana [μιά παραμάνα]
sail: can we go sailing? boroomeh na pameh varkatha? [μπορούμε να πάμε βαρκάδα;]
(in bigger yacht) boroomeh na pameh volta meh to yot? [μπορούμε να πάμε βόλτα με το γιώτ;]
sailboard ena 'windsurf' [ένα 'windsurf']
sailboarding: to go sailboarding pao ya 'windsurf' [πάω για 'windsurf']
sailor enas naftis [ένας ναύτης]
he's a keen sailor ineh fanatikos THalasoporos [είναι φανατικός θαλασσοπόρος]
salad mia salata [μιά σαλάτα]
salami ena salami [ένα σαλάμι]
sale: is it for sale? ineh ya poolima? [είναι για

πούλημα;]
salmon o solomos [ο σολομός]
salt to alati [το αλάτι]
same ithios [ίδιος]
the same again, please to ithio ksana, parakalo [το ίδιο ξανά, παρακαλώ]
it's all the same to me to ithio moo kani [το ίδιο μου κάνει]
sand i amos [η άμμος]
sandals ta santhalia [τα σανδάλια]
sandwich ena 'sandwich' [ένα σάντουϊτς]
a ham/cheese sandwich ena 'sandwich' meh zambon/tiri [ένα σάντουϊτς με ζαμπόν/τυρί]
sanitary towels i servi-etes [οι σερβιέτες]
satisfactory ikanopi-itikos [ικανοποιητικός]
Saturday savato [Σάββατο]
sauce i saltsa [η σάλτσα]
saucepan ena tigani [ένα τηγάνι]
saucer ena piataki [ένα πιατάκι]
sauna mia saoona [μιά σάουνα]
sausage ena lookaniko [ένα λουκάνικο]
say leo [λέω]
how do you say...in Greek? pos leneh sta elinika...? [πώς λένε στα Ελληνικά...;]
what did he say? ti ipeh? [τί είπε;]
scarf *(for head)* ena mandili [ένα μαντήλι]
(for neck) ena kaskol [ένα κασκόλ]
scenery i THea [η θέα]
schedule to programa [το πρόγραμμα]
on schedule stin ora too [στην ώρα του]
behind schedule eKHi kaTHisterisi [έχει καθυστερήσει]
scheduled flight mia programatismeni ptisi [μιά προγραμματισμένη πτήση]
school to sKHolio [το σχολείο]
scissors: a pair of scissors ena psalithi [ένα ψαλίδι]

scooter ena skooter [ένα σκούτερ]
Scotland i skotia [η Σκωτία]
Scottish skotsezikos [Σκωτσέζικος]
scream *(verb)* fonazo [φωνάζω]
(noun) mia kravyi [μιά κραυγή]
screw i vitha [η βίδα]
screwdriver ena katsavithi [ένα κατσαβίδι]
sea i THalasa [η θάλασσα]
by the sea konda sti THalasa [κοντά στη θάλασσα]
seafood ta THalasina [τα θαλασσινά]
search *(verb)* psaKHno [ψάχνω]
search party mia omatha erevnas [μιά ομάδα έρευνας]
seasick: I get seasick i THalasa meh anakatevi [η θάλασσα με ανακατεύει]
seaside i paralia [η παραλία]
season i epoKHi [η εποχή]
in the high season tin periotho eKHmis [την περίοδο αιχμής]
in the low season ti nekri periotho [τη νεκρή περίοδο]
seasoning ta baKHarika [τα μπαχαρικά]
seat mia THesi [μιά θέση]
is this somebody's seat? ineh piasmeni afti i THesi? [είναι πιασμένη αυτή η θέση;]
seat belt i zoni asfalias [η ζώνη ασφαλείας]

✈ Wearing a seat belt is compulsory in Greece.

sea-urchin enas aKHinos [ένας αχινός]
seaweed to fiki [το φύκι]
second *(adjective)* thefteros [δεύτερος]
(of time) ena thefterolepto [ένα δευτερόλεπτο]
on the second of... *(date)* stis thio too... [στις δύο του...]
secondhand apo theftero KHeri [από δεύτερο χέρι]

see vlepo [βλέπω]
have you seen...? ithateh...? [είδατε...;]
can I see the room? boro na tho to thomatio? [μπορώ να δω το δωμάτιο;]
see you! ta lemeh! [τα λέμε!]
see you tonight THa seh tho to vrathi [θα σε δω το βράδυ]
oh, I see a, katalava [α, κατάλαβα]
self-catering apartment ena thiamerisma meh pliri thiatrofi [ένα διαμέρισμα με πλήρη διατροφή]
self-service to self-servis [το σελφ-σέρβις]
sell poolo [πουλώ]
send stelno [στέλνω]
I want to send this to England THelo na stilo afto stin anglia [θέλω να στείλω αυτό στην Αγγλία]
sensitive evesTHitos [ευαίσθητος]
separate *(adjective)* KHoristos [χωριστός]
I'm separated imeh seh thiastasi [είμαι σε διάσταση]
separately: can we pay separately? boroomeh na plirosoomeh KHorista? [μπορούμε να πληρώσουμε χωριστά;]
September septemvrios [Σεπτέμβριος]
serious sovaros [σοβαρός]
I'm serious to leo sovara [το λέω σοβαρά]
this is serious afto ineh sovaro [αυτό είναι σοβαρό]
is it serious, doctor? ineh sovaro, yatreh? [είναι σοβαρό, γιατρέ;]
service: is service included? simberilamvaneteh to servis? [συμπεριλαμβάνεται το σέρβις;]
service station ena venzinathiko [ένα βενζινάδικο]
serviette mia petseta fayitoo [μιά πετσέτα φαγητού]
several meriki [μερικοί]

sex to seks [το σεξ]
sexy seksi [σέξυ]
shade: in the shade sti skia [στη σκιά]
shake koono [κουνώ]
to shake hands andalaso KHirapsia [ανταλάσσω χειραψία]

✈ Customary to shake hands when you meet someone and when you leave them.

shallow riKHos [ρηχός]
shame: what a shame! ti krima! [τι κρίμα!]
shampoo ena sampooan [ένα σαμπουάν]
shandy mia bira meh lemonatha [μιά μπύρα με λεμονάδα]

✈ A strange thing to ask for in Greece.

share mirazomeh [μοιράζομαι]
shark enas karkHarias [ένας καρχαρίας]
sharp kofteros [κοφτερός]
(taste, pain) thinatos [δυνατός]
shave ksirizo [ξυρίζω]
shaver mia ksiristiki miKHani [μιά ξυριστική μηχανή]
shaving foam mia krema ksirismatos [μιά κρέμα ξυρίσματος]
shaving point mia priza ksiristikis miKHanis [μιά πρίζα ξυριστικής μηχανής]
she afti [αυτή]

If there is no special emphasis Greek doesn't use the word **afti**.
she is tired ineh koorasmeni [είναι κουρασμένη]

sheet ena sendoni [ένα σεντόνι]
shelf to rafi [το ράφι]
shell *(sea-)* ena kelifos [ένα κέλυφος]
shellfish ta ostrako-ithi [τα οστρακοειδή]

shelter *(place)* to katafiyio [το καταφύγιο]
can we shelter here? boroomeh na profilaKHtoomeh etho? [μπορούμε να προφυλαχτούμε εδώ;]
sherry ena seri [ένα σέρρυ]
ship to plio [το πλοίο]
shirt ena pookamiso [ένα πουκάμισο]
shit! skata! [σκατά!]
shock ena sok [σοκ]
I got an electric shock from the... meh tinakseh to revma too... [με τίναξε το ρεύμα του...]
shock-absorber to amortiser [το αμορτισέρ]
shoelaces ta korthonia [τα κορδόνια]
shoes ta papootsia [τα παπούτσια]

✈									
men:				40	41	42	43	44	45
women:	36	37	38	39	40	41			
UK:	3	4	5	6	7	8	9	10	11

shop to magazi [το μαγαζί]
shop assistant o/i ipalilos too katastimatos [ο/η υπάλληλος του καταστήματος]
shopping: I've some shopping to do eKHo na kano merika psonia [έχω να κάνω μερικά ψώνια]

✈ Open from 8 am to 1.30 pm and then from 5 pm to 8.30 pm Mon-Fri; on Saturdays open only in the morning; different in touristy areas.

short kondos [κοντός]
short cut enas sindomos thromos [ένας σύντομος δρόμος]
shorts to sorts [το σορτς]
shoulder o omos [ο ώμος]
shout fonazo [φωνάζω]
show: please show me parakalo, thikseh moo [παρακαλώ, δείξε μου]

shower: with shower meh doos [με ντους]
shrimps i garithes [οι γαρίδες]
shut klistos [κλειστός]
they're shut ineh klista [είναι κλειστά]
when do you shut? poteh klineteh? [πότε κλείνετε;]
shut up! skaseh! [σκάσε!]
shy dropalos [ντροπαλός]
sick arostos [άρρωστος]
I feel sick anakatevomeh [ανακατεύομαι]
he's been sick ekaneh emeto [έκανε εμετό]
side i plevra [η πλευρά]
by the side of the road stin akri too thromoo [στην άκρη του δρόμου]
side street ena thromaki [ένα δρομάκι]
sight: the sights of... ta aksioTHeata too... [τα αξιοθέατα του...]
sightseeing tour mia ekthromi sta aksioTHeh-ata [μιά εκδρομή στα αξιοθέατα]
sign *(notice)* i pinakitha [η πινακίδα]
signal: he didn't signal then ekaneh sima [δεν έκανε σήμα]
signature i ipografi [η υπογραφή]
silence i siopi [η σιωπή]
silencer i eksatmisi [η εξάτμιση]
silk to metaksi [το μετάξι]
silly ano-itos [ανόητος]
silver to asimi [το ασήμι]
similar omios [όμοιος]
simple aplos [απλός]
since: since last week apo tin perasmeni evthomatha [απο την περασμένη εβδομάδα]
since we arrived apo toteh poo ftasameh [από τότε που φτάσαμε]
(because) epithi [επειδή]
sincere ilikrinis [ειλικρινής]
sing tragootho [τραγουδώ]

single: I'm single imeh elefTHeros/elefTHeri [είμαι ελεύθερος/ελεύθερη]
a single to... ena aplo ya... [ένα απλό για...]
single room ena mono thomatio [ένα μονό δωμάτιο]
sister: my sister i athelfi moo [η αδελφή μου]
sit: can I sit here? boro na *kaTHiso* etho? [μπορώ να καθήσω εδώ;]
size to meyeTHos [το μέγεθος]
(of shoes) to noomero [το νούμερο]
ski to ski [το σκι]
skid glistro [γλυστρώ]
skin to therma [το δέρμα]
skin-diving i ipovriKHia kolibisi [η υποβρύχια κολύμπηση]

✈ Use of an aqualung requires a police permit.

skirt mia foosta [μιά φούστα]
sky o ooranos [ο ουρανός]
sleep: I can't sleep then boro na *kimiTHo* [δεν μπορώ να κοιμηθώ]
sleeper *(rail)* to vagon li [το βαγκόν λη]
sleeping bag ena slipin bag [ένα σλίπινγκ μπαγκ]
sleeping pill ena ipnotiko KHapi [ένα υπνωτικό χάπι]
sleeve to maniki [το μανίκι]
slide *(photo)* ena 'slide' [ένα σλάιντ]
slow argos [αργός]
could you speak a little slower? boriteh na milateh ligo pio arga? [μπορείτε να μιλάτε λίγο πιό αργά;]
slowly arga [αργά]
small mikros [μικρός]
smaller notes KHartonomismata mikroteris aksias [χαρτονομίσματα μικρότερης αξίας]
small change ta psila [τα ψιλά]

smell: there's a funny smell mirizi peri-erga [μυρίζει περίεργα]
it smells vroma-i [βρωμάει]
smile *(verb)* KHamoyelo [χαμογελώ]
smoke o kapnos [ο καπνός]
do you smoke? kapnizeteh? [καπνίζετε;]
can I smoke? boro na kapniso? [μπορώ να καπνίσω;]

✈ Smoking is prohibited in most public buildings and on public transport.

snack enas mezes [ένας μεζές]
can we just have a snack? boroomeh na tsimbisoomeh kati? [μπορούμε να τσιμπήσουμε κάτι;]

✈ Try **ena soovlaki** [ένα σουβλάκι] meat and salad in pitta bread. Or a cheese pie, **mia tiropita** [μιά τυρόπιτα].

snake ena fithi [ένα φίδι]
snorkel enas anapnefstiras [ένας αναπνευστήρας]
snow to KHioni [το χιόνι]
so: it's so hot today kani tosi zesti simera [κάνει τόση ζέστη σήμερα]
not so much oKHi toso poli [όχι τόσο πολύ]
so am I ki ego [κι εγώ]
so do I ki ego [κι εγώ]
soap to sapooni [το σαπούνι]
soap powder to aporipandiko [το απορρυπαντικό]
sober ksemeTHistos [ξεμέθυστος]
socks i kaltses [οι κάλτσες]
soda (water) mia sotha [μιά σόδα]
soft drink ena anapsiktiko [ένα αναψυκτικό]
sole i sola [η σόλα]
some: some people meriki anTHropi [μερικοί άνθρωποι]
can I have some? boro na eKHo liga? [μπορώ να

έχω λίγα;]
some bread ligo psomi [λίγο ψωμί]
some beer liyi bira [λίγη μπύρα]
somebody kapios [κάποιος]
something kati [κάτι]
sometimes kamia fora [καμιά φορά]
somewhere kapoo [κάπου]
son: my son o yos moo [ο γιός μου]
song ena tragoothi [ένα τραγούδι]
soon sindoma [σύντομα]
as soon as possible oso to thinato sindomotera [όσο το δυνατό συντομότερα]
sooner pio noris [πιό νωρίς]
sore: it's sore pona-i [πονάει]
sore throat o ponolemos [ο πονόλαιμος]
sorry: (I'm) sorry lipameh [λυπάμαι]
sorry? signomi? [συγγνώμη;]
sort: this sort afto to ithos [αυτό το είδος]
what sort of...? ti ithos...? [τί είδος...;]
will you sort it out? THa to kanoniseteh? [θα το κανονίσετε;]
so-so etsi ki etsi [έτσι κι έτσι]
soup i soopa [η σούπα]
sour ksinos [ξινός]
south o notos [ο νότος]
South Africa i notios afriki [η Νότιος Αφρική]
souvenir ena enTHimio [ένα ενθύμιο]
spade ena ftiari [ένα φτυάρι]
(child's) ena ftiaraki [ένα φτυαράκι]
Spain i ispania [η Ισπανία]
spare part ena andalaktiko [ένα ανταλλακτικό]
spare wheel i rezerva [η ρεζέρβα]
spark plug ena boozi [ένα μπουζί]
speak milao [μιλάω]
do you speak English? milateh anglika? [μιλάτε Αγγλικά;]
I don't speak Greek then milao elinika

[δεν μιλάω Ελληνικά]
special ithi-eteros [ιδιαίτερος]
specialist enas/mia ithikos [ένας/μιά ειδικός]
spectacles ta yalia [τα γυαλιά]
speed i taKHitita [η ταχύτητα]
he was speeding etreKHeh [έτρεχε]
speed limit to orio taKHititos [το όριο ταχύτητος]

✈ 100 kph (62 mph) is the maximum on motorways with 40 kph (25 mph) in town.

speedometer to konder [το κοντέρ]
spend *(money)* ksothevo [ξοδεύω]
spice ena baKHariko [ένα μπαχαρικό]
is it spicy? ineh pikandiko? [είναι πικάντικο;]
spider mia araKHni [μιά αράχνη]
spoon ena kootali [ένα κουτάλι]
sprain: I've sprained my... strabooliksa to...moo [στραμπούληξα το...μου]
spring *(of car, seat)* to elatirio [το ελατήριο] *(season)* i aniksi [η άνοιξη]
square *(in town)* i platia [η πλατεία]
two square metres thio tetragonika metra [δύο τετραγωνικά μέτρα]
stairs i skales [οι σκάλες]
stalls i platia [η πλατεία]
stamp ena gramatosimo [ένα γραμματόσημο]
two stamps for England thio gramatosima ya tin anglia [δύο γραμματόσημα για την Αγγλία]
stand *(at fair)* o pangos [ο πάγκος]
stand-by: to fly stand-by beno seh lista anamonis [μπαίνω σε λίστα αναμονής]
star to astro [το άστρο]
starboard i theksia plevra too plioo [η δεξιά πλευρά του πλοίου]
start: when does it start? poteh arKHizi? [πότε αρχίζει;]
my car won't start to aftokinito moo then

ksekina-i [το αυτοκίνητό μου δεν ξεκινάει]
starter *(of car)* i miza [η μίζα]
(food) ena orektiko [ένα ορεκτικό]
starving: I'm starving peTHeno tis pinas [πεθαίνω της πείνας]
station o staTHmos [ο σταθμός]
statue ena agalma [ένα άγαλμα]
stay: we enjoyed our stay i *thiamoni* mas itan poli efkHaristi [η διαμονή μας ήταν πολύ ευχάριστη]
stay there mineh eki [μείνε εκεί]
I'm staying at... meno sto... [μένω στο...]
steak mia brizola [μιά μπριζόλα]

YOU MAY HEAR
pos ti THeleteh? *how would you like it done?*
kala psimeni *well done*
misopsimeni *medium*
oKHi poli psimeni *rare*

✈ If you ask for a rare steak, it will be almost raw!

steal: my wallet's been stolen moo *klepsaneh* to portofoli [μου κλέψανε το πορτοφόλι]
steep apotomos [απότομος]
steering to sistima thi-efTHinsis [το σύστημα διεύθυνσης]
steering wheel to timoni [το τιμόνι]
step *(of stairs)* to skali [το σκαλί]
sterling i sterlina [η στερλίνα]
stewardess i aerosinothos [η αεροσυνοδός]
sticking plaster ena lefkoplast [ένα λευκοπλάστ]
sticky kolothis [κολλώδης]
stiff aliyistos [αλύγιστος]
still: keep still stasoo akinitos [στάσου ακίνητος]
I'm still here imeh akomi etho [είμαι ακόμη εδώ]
I'm still waiting akoma perimeno [ακόμα περιμένω]

sting: I've been stung by a... meh tsimbiseh mia... [με τσίμπησε μιά...]
stink mia vroma [μιά βρώμα]
it stinks vroma-i asKHima [βρωμάει άσχημα]
stomach to stomaKHi [το στομάχι]
have you got something for an upset stomach? eKHeteh kanena farmako ya pono stomaKHoo? [έχετε κανένα φάρμακο για πόνο στομάχου;]
stomach-ache: I have a stomach-ache pona-i to stomaKHi moo [πονάει το στομάχι μου]
stone mia petra [μιά πέτρα]

✈ 1 stone = 6.35 kilos

stop *(for bus)* i stasi [η στάση]
stop! stamata! [σταμάτα!]
do you stop near...? stamatateh konda sti...? [σταματάτε κοντά στη...;]
could you stop here? boriteh na stamatiseteh etho? [μπορείτε να σταματήσετε εδώ;]
stop-over mia enthiamesi stasi [μιά ενδιάμεση στάση]
storm mia THi-ela [μιά θύελλα]
straight efTHis [ευθύς]
go straight on piyeneteh efTHia [πηγαίνετε ευθεία]
a straight whisky ena sketo ooiski [ένα σκέτο ουΐσκι]
straightaway amesos [αμέσως]
strange *(odd)* paraksenos [παράξενος]
(unknown) agnostos [άγνωστος]
stranger enas ksenos [ένας ξένος]
(woman) mia kseni [μιά ξένη]
I'm a stranger here imeh ksenos/kseni etho [είμαι ξένος/ξένη εδώ]
strawberry mia fraoola [μιά φράουλα]
street o thromos [ο δρόμος]

street map enas othikos KHartis [ένας οδικός χάρτης]
string: have you got any string? eKHeteh kaTHoloo *spango?* [έχετε καθόλου σπάγγο;]
stroke: he's had a stroke epaTHeh apopliksia [έπαθε αποπληξία]
strong thinatos [δυνατός]
stuck *(drawer etc)* frakarismenos [φρακαρισμένος]
student enas fititis [ένας φοιτητής]
(female) mia fititria [μιά φοιτήτρια]
stupid vlakas [βλάκας]
such: such a lot tosa pola [τόσα πολλά]
suddenly ksafnika [ξαφνικά]
sugar i zaKHari [η ζάχαρη]
suit *(man's)* ena koostoomi [ένα κουστούμι]
(woman's) ena tayer [ένα ταγιέρ]
suitable katalilos [κατάλληλος]
suitcase mia valitsa [μιά βαλίτσα]
summer to kalokeri [το καλοκαίρι]
sun o ilios [ο ήλιος]
in the sun ston ilio [στον ήλιο]
out of the sun sti skia [στη σκιά]
sunbathe kano ilioTHerapia [κάνω ηλιοθεραπεία]
sun block ena andiliako [ένα αντηλιακό]
sunburn to engavma apo ton ilio [το έγκαυμα από τον ήλιο]
sun cream mia krema ya ton ilio [μιά κρέμα για τον ήλιο]
Sunday kiriaki [Κυριακή]
sunglasses ta yalia ilioo [τα γυαλιά ηλίου]
sun lounger mia shez long [μιά σεζ-λονγκ]
sunstroke i iliasi [η ηλίαση]
suntan to mavrisma apo ton ilio [το μαύρισμα από τον ήλιο]
suntan oil ena lathi ilioo [ένα λάδι ηλίου]
supermarket to 'supermarket' [το σούπερ μάρκετ]
supper to thipno [το δείπνο]

sure: I'm not sure then imeh veveos/veveh-i [δεν είμαι βέβαιος/βέβαιη]
sure! veveos! [βεβαίως!]
surfboard mia sanitha ya serfin [μιά σανίδα για σέρφινγκ]
surfing: to go surfing pao ya serfin [πάω για σέρφινγκ]
surname to epiTHeto [το επίθετο]
swearword mia vrisia [μιά βρισιά]
sweat *(verb)* ithrono [ιδρώνω]
sweater ena poolover [ένα πουλόβερ]
sweet *(dessert)* ena epithorpio [ένα επιδόρπιο]
(wine) glikos [γλυκός]
it's too sweet ineh poli gliko [είναι πολύ γλυκό]
sweets i karameles [οι καραμέλες]
swerve: I had to swerve eprepeh na pareklino [έπρεπε να παρεκκλίνω]
swim: I'm going for a swim pao ya kolibi [πάω για κολύμπι]
I can't swim then ksero kolibi [δεν ξέρω κολύμπι]
let's go for a swim pameh ya kolibi [πάμε για κολύμπι]
swimming costume to mayo [το μαγιό]
swimming pool i pisina [η πισίνα]
switch o thiakoptis [ο διακόπτης]
to switch on anavo [ανάβω]
to switch off svino [σβήνω]
Switzerland i elvetia [η Ελβετία]

T

table to trapezi [το τραπέζι]
a table for four ena trapezi ya teseris [ένα τραπέζι για τέσσερεις]
table wine ena epitrapezio krasi [ένα επιτραπέζιο κρασί]

take perno [παίρνω]
can I take this? boro na to paro afto? [μπορώ να το πάρω αυτό;]
will you take me to the airport? boriteh na meh pareteh sto a-erothromio? [μπορείτε να με πάρετε στο αεροδρόμιο;]
how long will it take? posi ora THa pari? [πόση ώρα θα πάρει;]
somebody has taken my bags kapios *pireh* tis valitses moo [κάποιος πήρε τις βαλίτσες μου]
can I take you out tonight? THelis na seh paro ekso simera to vrathi? [θέλεις να σε πάρω έξω σήμερα το βράδυ;]
is this seat taken? ineh *katilimeni* afti i THesi? [είναι κατειλημμένη αυτή η θέση;]
I'll take it THa to agoraso [θα το αγοράσω]
talk *(verb)* milao [μιλάω]
tall psilos [ψηλός]
tampons ta tambon [τα ταμπόν]
tan to mavrisma [το μαύρισμα]
I want to get a tan THelo na mavriso [θέλω να μαυρίσω]
tank *(of car etc)* to depozito [το ντεπόζιτο]
tap i vrisi [η βρύση]
tape *(cassette)* mia kaseta [μιά κασέτα]
tape-recorder to magnitofono [το μαγνητόφωνο]
tariff i tarifa [η ταρίφα]
taste i yefsi [η γεύση]
(in clothes etc) to goosto [το γούστο]
can I taste it? boro na to *thokimaso*? [μπορώ να το δοκιμάσω;]
taxi ena taksi [ένα ταξί]
will you get me a taxi? THa moo kaleseteh ena taksi? [θα μου καλέσετε ένα ταξί;]
where can I get a taxi? poo boro na vro ena taksi? [πού μπορώ να βρω ένα ταξί;]

✈ Taxis are fairly cheap, especially in Athens. But they'll charge double for a hire between 1 am and 6 am as well as for going outside city boundaries. Surcharges also apply if you are entering a ferry port or airport or are carrying a lot of luggage. Out of town, some taxis won't have meters, and you'll have to agree on a price with the taxi-driver.

taxi-driver o taksitzis [ο ταξιτζής]
(female) i taksitzoo [η ταξιτζού]
tea ena tsa-i [ένα τσάι]
could I have a cup of tea? boro na eKHo ena flitzani tsa-i? [μπορώ να έχω ένα φλυτζάνι τσάι;]
could I have a pot of tea? boro na eKHo mia tsayera tsa-i? [μπορώ να έχω μία τσαγιέρα τσάι;]

✈ Tea is normally served black or with lemon; tea with milk is very unusual and milk must be ordered separately.

with lemon? meh lemoni? [με λεμόνι;]
no, with milk, please oKHi, meh gala, parakalo [όχι, με γάλα, παρακαλώ]

teach: could you teach me some Greek? boris na meh *thithaksis* liga elinika? [μπορείς να με διδάξεις λίγα Ελληνικά;]
teacher o thaskalos [ο δάσκαλος]
(woman) i thaskala [η δασκάλα]
telephone to tilefono [το τηλέφωνο]
go to **phone**
telephone directory o tilefonikos katalogos [ο τηλεφωνικός κατάλογος]
television i tileorasi [η τηλεόραση]
I'd like to watch television THa iTHela na tho tileorasi [θα ήθελα να δω τηλεόραση]

tell: could you tell me where...? boriteh na moo *piteh* poo...? [μπορείτε να μου πείτε πού...;]
could you tell him...? boriteh na too piteh...? [μπορείτε να του πείτε...;]
I told him that... too ipa oti... [του είπα ότι...]
temperature *(weather etc)* i THermokrasia [η θερμοκρασία]
he's got a temperature eKHi pireto [έχει υρετό]
temple o naos [ο ναός]
tennis to tenis [το τέννις]
tennis ball mia bala too tenis [μιά μπάλλα του τέννις]
tennis court ena yipetho too tenis [ένα γήπεδο του τέννις]
tennis racket mia raketa too tenis [μιά ρακέτα του τέννις]
tent i tenda [η τέντα]
terminus to terma [το τέρμα]
terrible foveros [φοβερός]
terrific ekseretikos [εξαιρετικός]
text: I'll text you THa soo stilo minima sto kinito [θα σου στείλω μήνυμα στο κινητό]
text message ena minima sto kinito [ένα μήνυμα στο κινητό]
than apo [από]
bigger than... megaliteros apo... [μεγαλύτερος από...]
thanks, thank you efkHaristo [ευχαριστώ]
thank you very much efkHaristo poli [ευχαριστώ πολύ]
no thank you oKHi, efkHaristo [όχι, ευχαριστώ]
thank you for your help efkHaristo ya ti vo-iTHia sas [ευχαριστώ για τη βοήθειά σας]

YOU MAY THEN HEAR
parakalo *you're welcome*

that: that... ekinos o.../ekini i.../ekino to...

[εκείνος ο.../εκείνη η.../εκείνο το...]

> Three forms depending on whether the noun is **o/i/to**.

that man/that table ekinos o andras/ekino to trapezi [εκείνος ο άντρας/εκείνο το τραπέζι]
I would like that one THa iTHela ekino [θα ήθελα εκείνο]
and that? keh afto? [και αυτό;]
I think that... nomizo oti... [νομίζω ότι...]
the o/i/to [ο/η/το]; *(plural)* i/i/ta [οι/οι/τα]

> The corresponding words for 'a' are **enas/mia/ena** [ένας/μιά/ένα].

theatre to THeatro [το θέατρο]
their

> To say 'their...' you wrap the Greek for 'the' (either of **o/i/to**) and the word **toos** around what is theirs.
> **their son** o yos toos [ο γιός τους]

theirs thikos toos [δικός τους]
them toos/tis/ta [τους/τις/τα]

> Depends on whether the word replaced by 'them' is used with **o/i/to**.

then *(at that time)* toteh [τότε]
(after that) katopin [κατόπιν]
there eki [εκεί]
how do I get there? pos THa pao eki? [πώς θα πάω εκεί;]
is there/are there...? iparKHi/iparKHoon...? [υπάρχει/υπάρχουν...;]
there is/there are... iparKHi/iparKHoon... [υπάρχει/υπάρχουν...]
there isn't/there aren't... then iparKHi/then iparKHoon... [δεν υπάρχει/δεν υπάρχουν...]

there you are *(giving something)* oristeh [ορίστε]
these afti i.../aftes i.../afta ta... [αυτοί οι.../αυτές οι.../αυτά τα...]

> Three forms depending on whether the noun is used with **o/i/to**.

these apples afta ta mila [αυτά τα μήλα]
can I take these? boro na ta paro afta? [μπορώ να τα πάρω αυτά;]
they afti/aftes/afta [αυτοί/αυτές/αυτά]

> Depends on whether the word 'they' refers to is used with **o/i/to**.
> If there is no special emphasis Greek doesn't use any word for 'they'.
> **where are they?** poo ineh? [πού είναι;]

thick pakHis [παχύς]
(stupid) KHazos [χαζός]
thief o kleftis [ο κλέφτης]
(female) i kleftra [η κλέφτρα]
thigh o miros [ο μηρός]
thin athinatos [αδύνατος]
thing ena pragma [ένα πράγμα]
I've lost all my things eKHasa ola moo ta pragmata [έχασα όλα μου τα πράγματα]
think skeptomeh [σκέπτομαι]
I'll think it over THa to skefto [θα το σκεφτώ]
I think so nomizo [νομίζω]
I don't think so then nomizo [δεν νομίζω]
third *(adjective)* tritos [τρίτος]
thirsty: I'm thirsty thipsao [διψάω]
this: this... aftos o.../afti i.../afto to... [αυτός ο.../αυτή η.../αυτό το...]

> Three forms depending on whether the noun is used with **o/i/to**.

this hotel/this street afto to ksenothoKHio/aftos

o thromos [αυτό το ξενοδοχείο/αυτός ο δρόμος]
can I have this one? boro na ekho afto etho? [μπορώ να έχω αυτό εδώ;]
this is my wife/this is Mr... afti ineh i yineka moo/aftos ineh o kirios... [αυτή είναι η γυναίκα μου/αυτός είναι ο κύριος...]
this is very good afto ineh poli kalo [αυτό είναι πολύ καλό]
this is... *(on telephone)* legomeh... [λέγομαι...]
is this...? afto ineh...? [αυτό είναι...;]
and this? keh afto? [και αυτό;]
those: those... ekini i.../ekines i.../ekina ta... [εκείνοι οι.../εκείνες οι.../εκείνα τα...]

> Three forms depending on whether the noun is used with **o/i/to**.

no, not these, those okhi, okhi afta, ekina [όχι, όχι αυτά, εκείνα]
thread i klosti [η κλωστή]
throat o lemos [ο λαιμός]
throttle *(of motorbike, boat)* i valvitha [η βαλβίδα]
through *(across)* thia mesoo [διά μέσου]
through Corinth meso tis korinthoo [μέσω της Κορίνθου]
throw rikhno [ρίχνω]
thumb o andikhiras [ο αντίχειρας]
thunder i vrondi [η βροντή]
thunderstorm i kateyitha meh keravnoos [η καταιγίδα με κεραυνούς]
Thursday pempti [Πέμπτη]
ticket to isitirio [το εισιτήριο]
(for cloakroom) o arithmos [ο αριθμός]
tie *(necktie)* i gravata [η γραβάτα]
tight *(clothes)* stenos [στενός]
tights to kaltson [το καλτσόν]
time o khronos [ο χρόνος]

I haven't got time then eкно кнrono [δεν έχω χρόνο]
for the time being pros to paron [προς το παρόν]
this time afti ti fora [αυτή τη φορά]
next time tin epomeni fora [την επόμενη φορά]
three times tris fores [τρεις φορές]
have a good time! kali thiaskethasi! [καλή διασκέδαση!]
what's the time? ti ora ineh? [τί ώρα είναι;]

HOW TO TELL THE TIME
it's one o'clock ineh mia i ora [είναι μία η ώρα]
it's two/three/four/five o'clock ineh thio/tris/teseris/pendeh i ora [είναι δύο/τρει/τέσσερι/πέντε η ώρα]
it's 5/10/20/25 past seven ineh epta keh pendeh/theka/ikosi/ikosi pendeh [είναι επτά και πέντε/δέκα/είκοσι/είκοσι πέντε]
it's quarter past eight/eight fifteen ineh okto keh tetarto/okto keh theka pendeh [είναι οκτώ και τέταρτο/οκτώ και δέκα πέντε]
it's half past nine/nine thirty ineh enea keh misi/enea keh trianda [είναι εννέα και μισή/εννέα και τριάντα]
it's 25/20/10/5 to ten ineh theka para ikosi pendeh/ikosi/theka/pendeh [είναι δέκα παρά είκοσι πέντε/είκοσι/δέκα/πέντε]
it's quarter to eleven/10.45 ineh endeka para tetarto/theka keh saranda pendeh [είναι έντεκα παρά τέταρτο/δέκα και σαράντα πέντε]
it's twelve o'clock (am/pm) ineh thotheka i ora (to proi/to vrathi) [είναι δώδεκα η ώρα (το πρωί/το βράδυ)]

at one o'clock stis mia i ora [στις μία η ώρα]
at three thirty stis tris keh trianda [στις τρεις και τριάντα]

timetable to programa [το πρόγραμμα]
tin *(can)* mia konserva [μιά κονσέρβα]
tin-opener ena anikHtiri [ένα ανοιχτήρι]
tip ena filothorima [ένα φιλοδώρημα]
is the tip included? perilamvaneteh to filothorima? [περιλαμβάνεται το φιλοδώρημα;]

✈ Usually included in the price in restaurants. Ushers in cinemas and theatres expect a tip but taxi-drivers don't.

tired koorasmenos [κουρασμένος]
tissues ta KHartomandila [τα χαρτομάντηλα]
to: to Heraklion sto iraklio [στο Ηράκλειο]
to England stin anglia [στην Αγγλία]
to our friends' sto spiti ton filon mas [στο σπίτι των φίλων μας]
go to **time**
toast *(piece of)* ena tost [ένα τοστ]
tobacco o kapnos [ο καπνός]
today simera [σήμερα]
toe to thaKHtilo too pothioo [το δάχτυλο του ποδιού]
together mazi [μαζί]
we're together imasteh mazi [είμαστε μαζί]
can we pay all together? boroomeh na plirosoomeh oli mazi? [μπορούμε να πληρώσουμε όλοι μαζί;]
toilet i tooaleta [η τουαλέτα]
where are the toilets? poo ineh i tooaleta? [πού είναι η τουαλέτα;]
I have to go to the toilet prepi na pao stin tooaleta [πρέπει να πάω στην τουαλέτα]

✈ It's ok to use the toilet in bars, cafés and hotels etc without asking. Dirty toilet paper goes in the wastebaskets not down the loo.

toilet paper: there's no toilet paper then iparKHi KHarti tooaletas [δεν υπάρχει χαρτί τουαλέτας]
tomato mia domata [μιά ντομάτα]
tomato juice ena domatozoomo [ένα ντοματόζουμο]
tomato ketchup i ketsap [η κέτσαπ]
tomorrow avrio [αύριο]
tomorrow morning avrio to pro-i [αύριο το πρωί]
tomorrow afternoon avrio to apoyevma [αύριο το απόγευμα]
tomorrow evening avrio to vrathi [αύριο το βράδυ]
the day after tomorrow meTHavrio [μεθαύριο]
see you tomorrow THa seh tho avrio [θα σε δω αύριο]
tongue i glosa [η γλώσσα]
tonic (water) ena tonik [ένα τόνικ]
tonight apopseh [απόψε]
tonsillitis i amigthalititha [η αμυγδαλίτιδα]
too poli [πολύ]
(also) episis [επίσης]
that's too much afto ineh para poli [αυτό είναι πάρα πολύ]
me too ki ego [κι εγώ]
tool ena ergalio [ένα εργαλείο]
tooth to thondi [το δόντι]
toothache: I've got toothache eKHo ponothondo [έχω πονόδοντο]
toothbrush mia othondovoortsa [μιά οδοντόβουρτσα]
toothpaste i othondokrema [η οδοντόκρεμα]
top: on top of pano apo [πάνω από]

on the top floor sto pano patoma [στο πάνω πάτωμα]
at the top stin korifi [στην κορυφή]
torch enas fakos [ένας φακός]
total to sinolo [το σύνολο]
tough *(meat)* skliros [σκληρός]
tour i periothia [η περιοδεία]
(of museum etc) i ksenayisi [η ξενάγηση]
we'd like to go on a tour of... THeloomeh na pameh periothia sto... [θέλουμε να πάμε περιοδεία στο...]
we're touring around periothevoomeh [περιοδεύουμε]
tourist enas tooristas [ένας τουρίστας]
(woman) mia tooristria [μιά τουρίστρια]
tourist office ena grafio toorismoo [ένα γραφείο τουρισμού]
tow *(verb)* rimoolko [ρυμουλκώ]
can you give me a tow? boriteh na meh rimoolkiseteh? [μπορείτε να με ρυμουλκήσετε;]
towards pros [προς]
towel mia petseta [μιά πετσέτα]
town i poli [η πόλη]
(smaller) i komopoli [η κωμόπολη]
in town stin poli [στην πόλη]
will you take me into town? boriteh na meh pareteh sto kendro? [μπορείτε να με πάρετε στο κέντρο;]
towrope ena sKHini rimoolkiseos [ένα σχοινί ρυμουλκήσεως]
traditional patroparathotos [πατροπαράδοτος]
a traditional Greek meal ena patroparathoto eliniko fayito [ένα πατροπαράδοτο Ελληνικό φαγητό]
traffic i kikloforia [η κυκλοφορία]
traffic jam i kikloforiaki simforisi [η κυκλοφοριακή συμφόρηση]

traffic lights ta fanaria trokHeas [τα φανάρια τροχαίας]
train to treno [το τρένο]

✈ Book in advance as trains tend to be crowded; train travel is slow.

trainers ta aTHlitika papootsia [τα αθλητικά παπούτσια]
train station o staTHmos ton trenon [ο σταθμός των τρένων]
tranquillizers ta iremistika [τα ηρεμιστικά]
translate metafrazo [μεταφράζω]
would you translate that for me? boriteh na moo to metafraseteh afto? [μπορείτε να μου το μεταφράσετε αυτό;]
travel taksithevo [ταξιδεύω]
travel agent's ena praktorio taksithion [ένα πρακτορείο ταξιδιών]
traveller's cheque mia taksithiotiki epitayi [μιά ταξιδιωτική επιταγή]
tree to thendro [το δέντρο]
tremendous *(very good)* THavmasios [θαυμάσιος]
trim: just a trim, please freskarisma mono, parakalo [φρεσκάρισμα μόνο, παρακαλώ]
trip *(journey)* ena taksithi [ένα ταξίδι]
(outing) i ekthromi [η εκδρομή]
we want to go on a trip to... THeloomeh na pameh ekthromi sto... [θέλουμε να πάμε εκδρομή στο...]
trouble ta provlimata [τα προβλήματα]
I'm having trouble with... eKHo provlimata meh... [έχω προβλήματα με...]
trousers to panteloni [το παντελόνι]
true aliTHinos [αληθινός]
it's not true then ineh aliTHia [δεν είναι αλήθεια]
trunks to mayo [το μαγιό]
try thokimazo [δοκιμάζω]

can I try it on? boro na to thokimaso? [μπορώ να το δοκιμάσω;]
T-shirt ena bloozaki [ένα μπλουζάκι]
Tuesday triti [Τρίτη]
tunnel to toonel [το τούνελ]
Turkey i toorkia [η Τουρκία]
Turkish *(adjective)* toorkikos [Τουρκικός]
Turkish delight to lookoomi [το λουκούμι]
turn: where do we turn off? poo THa stripsoomeh? [πού θα στρίψουμε;]
twice thio fores [δύο φορές]
twice as much ta thipla [τα διπλά]
twin beds thio krevatia [δύο κρεβάτια]
twin room ena thomatio meh thio krevatia [ένα δωμάτιο με δύο κρεβάτια]
typical tipikos [τυπικός]
tyre ena lastiKHo [ένα λάστιχο]
I need a new tyre KHriazomeh kenooryo lastiKHo [χρειάζομαι καινούριο λάστιχο]

✈ **tyre pressure**

lb/sq in	18	20	22	26	28	30
kg/sq cm	1.3	1.4	1.5	1.7	2	2.1

U

ugly asKHimos [άσχημος]
ulcer to elkos [το έλκος]
umbrella mia ombrela [μιά ομπρέλλα]
uncle: my uncle o THios moo [ο θείος μου]
uncomfortable avolos [άβολος]
unconscious anesTHitos [αναίσθητος]
he's unconscious eKHaseh tis esTHisis too [έχασε τις αισθήσεις του]
under apo kato [από κάτω]
underdone apsitos [άψητος]
underground *(rail)* o ipoyios [ο υπόγειος]

✈ The Athens metro is now fully operational and is far preferable to buses.

understand: I understand katalaveno [καταλαβαίνω]
I don't understand then katalaveno [δεν καταλαβαίνω]
do you understand? katalavenis? [καταλαβαίνεις;]
undo lino [λύνω]
unfriendly eKHTHrikos [εχθρικός]
unhappy thistiKHismenos [δυστυχισμένος]
United States i inomenes politi-es [οι Ηνωμένες Πολιτείες]
university to panepistimio [το Πανεπιστήμιο]
unleaded i amolivthi venzini [η αμόλυβδη βενζίνη]
unlock kseklithono [ξεκλειδώνω]
until meKHri [μέχρι]
until next year meKHri too KHronoo [μέχρι του χρόνου]
not until Tuesday oKHi meKHri tin triti [όχι μέχρι την Τρίτη]
unusual asiniTHistos [ασυνήθιστος]
up pano [πάνω]
he's not up yet then ksipniseh akomi [δεν ξύπνησε ακόμη]
what's up? ti simveni? [τί συμβαίνει;]
up there eki pano [εκεί πάνω]
upside-down ta pano kato [τα πάνω κάτω]
upstairs pano [πάνω]
urgent epigon [επείγον]
us mas [μας]
it's us emis imasteh [εμείς είμαστε]
USA i ipa [οι ΗΠΑ]
use: can I use...? boro na KHrisimopi-iso...? [μπορώ να χρησιμοποιήσω...;]

useful KHrisimos [χρήσιμος]
usual siniTHismenos [συνηθισμένος]
as usual opos siniTHos [όπως συνήθως]
usually siniTHos [συνήθως]
U-turn mia strofi epi topoo [μιά στροφή επί τόπου]

V

vacate *(room)* athiazo [αδειάζω]
vacation i thiakopes [οι διακοπές]
vaccination enas emvoliasmos [ένας εμβολιασμός]
vacuum flask to THermos [το θερμός]
valid engiros [έγκυρος]
how long is it valid for? ya poso isKHi-i? [για πόσο ισχύει;]
valley i kilatha [η κοιλάδα]
valuable politimos [πολύτιμος]
my valuables ta politima andikimena moo [τα πολύτιμα αντικείμενά μου]
value i aksia [η αξία]
van ena troKHospito [ένα τροχόσπιτο]
vanilla vanilia [βανίλια]
veal to mosKHarisio kreas [το μοσχαρίσιο κρέας]
vegetables ta laKHanika [τα λαχανικά]
vegetarian enas/mia KHortofagos [ένας/μιά χορτοφάγος]

✈ Few Greeks are vegetarians.

ventilator o anemistiras [ο ανεμιστήρας]
very poli [πολύ]
very much para poli [πάρα πολύ]
via thia mesoo [διά μέσου]
village ena KHorio [ένα χωριό]
vine i klimataria [η κληματαριά]
vinegar to ksithi [το ξύδι]
vineyard ena ampeli [ένα αμπέλι]
violent vi-eos [βίαιος]

visit episkeptomeh [επισκέπτομαι]
vodka mia votka [μιά βότκα]
voice i foni [η φωνή]
voltage to volt [το βολτ]

> ✈ 220 in Greece, as in the UK.

W

waist i mesi [η μέση]
wait: will we have to wait long? THa prepi na *perimenoomeh* poli? [θα πρέπει να περιμένουμε πολύ;]
wait for me perimeneh meh [περίμενέ με]
I'm waiting for a friend/my wife perimeno enan filo/ti yineka moo [περιμένω έναν φίλο/τη γυναίκα μου]
waiter to garson [το γκαρσόν]
waiter! garson! [γκαρσόν!]
waitress i garsona [η γκαρσόνα]
wake: will you wake me up at 7.30? boriteh na meh *ksipniseteh* stis efta keh misi? [μπορείτε να με ξυπνήσετε στις εφτά και μισή;]
Wales i ooalia [η Ουαλία]
walk: can we walk there? boroomeh na pameh eki perpatondas? [μπορούμε να πάμε εκεί περπατώντας;]
wall o tiKHos [ο τοίχος]
wallet to portofoli [το πορτοφόλι]
want: I want a... THelo ena... [θέλω ένα...]
I want to talk to... THelo na miliso ston... [θέλω να μιλήσω στον...]
what do you want? ti THelis? [τί θέλεις;]
I don't want to then THelo [δεν θέλω]
he/she wants to... THeli na... [θέλει να...]
war o polemos [ο πόλεμος]
warm KHliaros [χλιαρός]

warning mia pro-ithopiisi [μιά προειδοποίηση]
was

> Here is the past tense of the verb 'to be'.
> **I was** imoon [ήμουν]
> **you were** *(familiar)* isoon [ήσουν]
> **you were** *(polite)* isasteh [ήσαστε]
> **he/she/it was** itan [ήταν]
> **we were** imasteh [ήμαστε]
> **you were** *(plural)* isasteh [ήσαστε]
> **they were** itan [ήταν]

wash: can you wash these for me? boriteh na moo ta *plineteh* afta? [μπορείτε να μου τα πλύνετε αυτά;]
washbasin o niptiras [ο νιπτήρας]
washing machine to plindirio [το πλυντήριο]
washing powder to aporipandiko [το απορρυπαντικό]
washer *(for nut)* i rothela [η ροδέλα]
wasp mia sfika [μιά σφήκα]
watch *(wristwatch)* to rolo-i [το ρολόι]
will you watch my bags for me? THa boroosateh na moo *prosekseteh* tis tsandes? [θα μπορούσατε να μου προσέξετε τις τσάντες;]
watch out! prosekHeh! [πρόσεχε!]
water to nero [το νερό]
can I have some water? boro na ekHo ligo nero? [μπορώ να έχω λίγο νερό;]
hot and cold running water zesto keh krio trekHoomeno nero [ζεστό και κρύο τρεχούμενο νερό]

> ✈ In towns or on some of the smaller islands you're better drinking mineral water.

waterproof athiavrokHos [αδιάβροχος]
waterskiing to THalasio ski [το θαλάσσιο σκι]
way: it's this way ineh apo etho [είναι από εδώ]

it's that way ineh apo eki [είναι από εκεί]
do it this way kaneh to etsi [κάνε το έτσι]
no way! apokli-eteh! [αποκλείεται!]
is it on the way to...? ineh ston thromo ya tin...? [είναι στον δρόμο για την...;]
could you tell me the way to get to...? boriteh na moo piteh ton thromo ya tin...? [μπορείτε να μου πείτε τον δρόμο για την...;]
go to **where** *for answers*

we emis [εμείς]

> If there is no special emphasis Greek doesn't use the word **emis**.
> **we're English** imasteh angli [είμαστε 'Αγγλοι]

weak *(person)* athinamos [αδύναμος]

weather o keros [ο καιρός]
what filthy weather! ti apesios keros! [τί απαίσιος καιρός!]
what's the weather forecast? ti le-i to meteoroloyiko theltio? [τί λέει το μετεωρολογικό δελτίο;]

> *YOU MAY THEN HEAR*
> THa kani zesti *it's going to be hot*
> THa eKHi kafsona *there's going to be a heatwave*
> THa vreksi *it's going to rain*

website i istoselitha [η ιστοσελίδα]

Wednesday tetarti [Τετάρτη]

week mia evthomatha [μιά εβδομάδα]
a week today seh mia evthomatha apo simera [σε μία εβδομάδα από σήμερα]
a week tomorrow seh mia evthomatha apo avrio [σε μία εβδομάδα από αύριο]

weekend: at the weekend to savatokiriako [το Σαββατοκύριοκο]

weight to varos [το βάρος]
welcome: you're welcome parakalo [παρακαλώ]
well: I'm not feeling well then esTHanomeh kala [δεν αισθάνομαι καλά]
he's not well then ineh kala [δεν είναι καλά]
how are you? – very well, thanks ti kanis? – poli kala, efkHaristo [τί κάνεις; – πολύ καλά, ευχαριστώ]
you speak English very well milateh anglika poli kala [μιλάτε Αγγλικά πολύ καλά]
well, well! ya fandasoo! [για φαντάσου!]
Welsh ooalos [Ουαλός]
were *go to* **was**
west i thisi [η δύση]
West Indies i thitikes inthi-es [οι Δυτικές Ινδίες]
wet igros [υγρός]
(weather) vroKHeros [βροχερός]
wet suit mia forma katathiseos [μιά φόρμα καταδύσεως]
what? ti? [τί;]
what is that? ti ineh ekino? [τί είναι εκείνο;]
what for? ya pio logo? [για ποιό λόγο;]
what train? pio treno? [ποιό τρένο;]
wheel i rotha [η ρόδα]
wheel chair mia anapiriki karekla [μιά αναπηρική καρέκλα]
when? poteh? [πότε;]
when is breakfast? poteh ineh to proyevma? [πότε είναι το πρόγευμα;]
when we arrived otan fTHasameh [όταν φθάσαμε]
where? poo? [πού;]
where is...? poo ineh...? [πού είναι...;]

YOU MAY THEN HEAR
isia *straight on*
o thefteros thromos aristera *second left*

o protos thromos theksia *first right*
seh thio KHiliometra *two kilometres further on*
then ksero *I don't know*

which? pios? [ποιός;]
which one? pio apola? [ποιό απ'όλα;]

YOU MAY THEN HEAR
afto *this one*
ekino *that one*
ekino eki *that one over there*

whisky ena ooiski [ένα ουΐσκι]
white aspros [άσπρος]
white wine ena aspro krasi [ένα άσπρο κρασί]
Whitsun i pendikosti [η Πεντηκοστή]
who? pios? [ποιός;]

YOU MAY THEN HEAR
aftos *him*
afti *her*

whose: whose is this? pianoo ineh afto? [ποιανού είναι αυτό;]

YOU MAY THEN HEAR
ineh too yani *it's John's*
ineh tis marias *it's Maria's*
ineh thiko moo *it's mine*

why? yati? [γιατί;]
why not? yati oKHi? [γιατί όχι;]

YOU MAY THEN HEAR
epithi *because*
etsi *just because*

wide platis [πλατύς]
wife: my wife i sizigos moo [η σύζυγός μου]
will: when will it be finished? poteh THa teliosi? [πότε θα τελειώσει;]

will you do it? boriteh na to kaneteh? [μπορείτε να το κάνετε;]

win kerthizo [κερδίζω]

who won? pios kerthiseh? [ποιός κέρδισε;]

wind o anemos [ο άνεμος]

window to paraTHiro [το παράθυρο]

(of shop) i vitrina [η βιτρίνα]

window seat mia THesi sto paraTHiro [μιά θέση στο παράθυρο]

windscreen to bar-priz [το μπαρ-πριζ]

windscreen wipers i ialokaTHaristires [οι υαλοκαθαριστήρες]

windy anemothis [ανεμώδης]

it's too windy fisa-i para poli [φυσάει πάρα πολύ]

wine to krasi [το κρασί]

can I see the wine list? boro na tho ton katalogo krasion? [μπορώ να δω τον κατάλογο κρασιών;]

two red wines thio potiria kokino krasi [δύο ποτήρια κόκκινο κρασί]

✈ Some wine terms:

aspro krasi [άσπρο κρασί] white wine
kokino krasi [κόκκινο κρασί] red wine
ksiros [ξηρός] dry
glikos [γλυκός] sweet
You could try:
retsina [ρετσίνα] resinated white wine, very strong and distinctive taste
mavrothafni [μαυροδάφνι] red dessert wine, very sweet
kokineli [κοκκινέλι] red wine sold on draught in 0.5 litre bottles
broosko [μπρούσκο] red and very dry

> **a bottle of house white/red** ena bookali spitiko aspro/kokino krasi [ένα μπουκάλι σπιτικό άσπρο/κόκκινο κρασί]

winter o KHimonas [ο χειμώνας]
wire to sirma [το σύρμα]
(electric) to kalothio [το καλώδιο]
wish: best wishes poles efKHes [πολλές ευχές]
with mazi [μαζί]
without KHoris [χωρίς]
witness enas/mia martiras [ένας/μιά μάρτυρας]
will you act as a witness for me? boriteh na isteh martiras moo? [μπορείτε να είστε μάρτυράς μου;]
woman i yineka [η γυναίκα]
women i yinekes [οι γυναίκες]
wonderful THavmasios [θαυμάσιος]
won't: it won't start then ksekina-i [δεν ξεκινάει]
wood to ksilo [το ξύλο]
(forest) to thasos [το δάσος]
wool to mali [το μαλλί]
word mia leksi [μιά λέξη]
I don't know that word then ksero afti ti leksi [δεν ξέρω αυτή τη λέξη]
work ergazomeh [εργάζομαι]
I work in London ergazomeh sto lonthino [εργάζομαι στο Λονδίνο]
it's not working then litooryi [δεν λειτουργεί]
worry: I'm worried about him anisiKHo yafton [ανησυχώ γι'αυτόν]
don't worry min anisiKHis [μην ανησυχείς]
worry beads to kombolo-i [το κομπολόι]
worse: it's worse ineh KHirotera [είναι χειρότερα]
worst o KHiroteros [ο χειρότερος]
worth: it's not worth that much then aksizi keh toso poli [δεν αξίζει και τόσο πολύ]
worthwhile: is it worthwhile going to...? aksizi

ton kopo na pameh sto...? [αξίζει τον κόπο να πάμε στο...;]

wrap: could you wrap it up? boriteh na to tilikseteh? [μπορείτε να το τυλίξετε;]

wrench *(tool)* ena klithi [ένα κλειδί]

wrist o karpos [ο καρπός]

write grafo [γράφω]

could you write it down? boriteh na moo to grapseteh? [μπορείτε να μου το γράψετε;]

I'll write to you THa soo grapso [θα σου γράψω]

writing paper to epistolokHarto [το επιστολόχαρτο]

wrong laTHos [λάθος]

I think the bill's wrong nomizo oti o logariasmos ineh laTHos [νομίζω ότι ο λογαριασμός είναι λάθος]

there's something wrong with... kati then pa-i kala meh... [κάτι δεν πάει καλά με...]

you're wrong kanis laTHos [κάνεις λάθος]

sorry, wrong number signomi, laTHos noomero [συγγνώμη, λάθος νούμερο]

what's wrong? ti simveni? [τί συμβαίνει;]

Y

yacht ena yot [ένα γιωτ]

yard

✈ 1 yard = 91.44 cms = 0.91 m

year o kHronos [ο χρόνος]

this year fetos [φέτος]

next year too kHronoo [του χρόνου]

yellow kitrinos [κίτρινος]

yellow pages o kHrisos othigos [ο χρυσός οδηγός]

yes neh [ναι]

yesterday KHTHes [χθες]
the day before yesterday proKHTHes [προχθές]
yesterday morning KHTHes to pro-i [χθες το πρωί]
yesterday afternoon KHTHes to apoyevma [χθες το απόγευμα]
yet: is it ready yet? ineh etimo? [είναι έτοιμο;]
not yet oKHi akoma [όχι ακόμα]
yoghurt ena yaoorti [ένα γιαούρτι]
you *(familiar singular)* esi [εσύ]
(polite or plural) esis [εσείς]

Use the familiar form when talking to children, young people or friends. Otherwise you should use the polite form.

If there is no special emphasis Greek doesn't use these words as subjects.
do you have...? eKHis...? [έχεις...;]
(polite or plural) eKHeteh...? [έχετε...;]
where are you? poo iseh [[πού είσαι;]
(polite or plural) poo isteh [[πού είστε;]

After a verb use:
(familiar singular) seh [σε]
(polite or plural) sas [σας]
I don't understand you then seh/sas katalaveno [δεν σε/σας καταλαβαίνω]
I'll send it to you THa soo/sas to stilo [θα σου/σας το στείλω]

After prepositions use:
(familiar singular) soo [σου]
(polite or plural) sas [σας]
with you mazi soo/sas [μαζί σου/σας]
for you ya soo/sas [για σου/σας]
without you KHoris soo/sas [χωρίς σου/σας]

Other uses:

is that you? esi iseh aftos? [εσύ είσαι αυτός;]

(polite or plural) esis isteh aftos? [εσείς είστε αυτός;]

who? – you pios? – esi/esis [ποιός; – εσύ/εσείς]

young neos [νέος]

your

To say 'your...' you wrap the Greek for 'the' (either of **o/i/to**) and the word **soo** or **sas** around what is yours.

(familiar singular) soo [σου]

(familiar or plural sas [σας]

is this your camera? afti ineh i fotografiki mikHani soo/sas? [αυτή είναι η φωτογραφική μηχανή σου/σας;]

your car/son to aftokinito soo/o yos soo [το αυτοκίνητό σου/ο γιός σου]

yours *(familiar singular)* thikos soo [δικός σου]
(familiar or plural) thikos sas [δικός σας]

youth hostel enas ksenonas neon [ένας ξενώνας νέων]

Z

zero mithen [μηδέν]

zip to fermooar [το φερμουάρ]

could you put a new zip on? boriteh na valeteh ena kenooryo fermooar? [μπορείτε να βάλετε ένα καινούριο φερμουάρ;]

Archipelago
GREECE
Mainland
CYPRUS
MACEDONIA
ALBANIA
Florina
Edessa
Kilkis
Gianitsa
Kastoria
Pela
Naousa
Ptolemaida
Langadas
Veria
Kozani
Vergina
Thessaloniki
Grevena
Corfu
Igoumenitsa
Katerini
Ioannina
Dodoni
Tirnavos
Paxi
Trikala
Larissa
Arta
Preveza
Karditsa
Volos
Lefkada
Karpenissi
Agrinio
Lamia
Ithaca
Kefalonia
Nafpaktos
Amfissa
Messolongi
Delfi
Livadia
Patra
Egio
Zante or Zakynthos
Halkida
Amaliada
Thiva
Pirgos
Platees
Olympia
Korinthos
Megara
Athina (Athens)
IONIO PELAGOS (IONIAN SEA)
Nemea
Mikines
Pireas
Argos
Rafina
Tripoli
Egina
Agia Marina
Nafplio
Epidavros
Messini
Poros
Sounio
Pilos
Kalamata
Sparti
Spetses
Hydra
Githio
EGEO PELAGOS (AEGEAN SEA)
N
W
E
S
Monemvassia
Potamos
Kithira
Kapsali
0 km 90

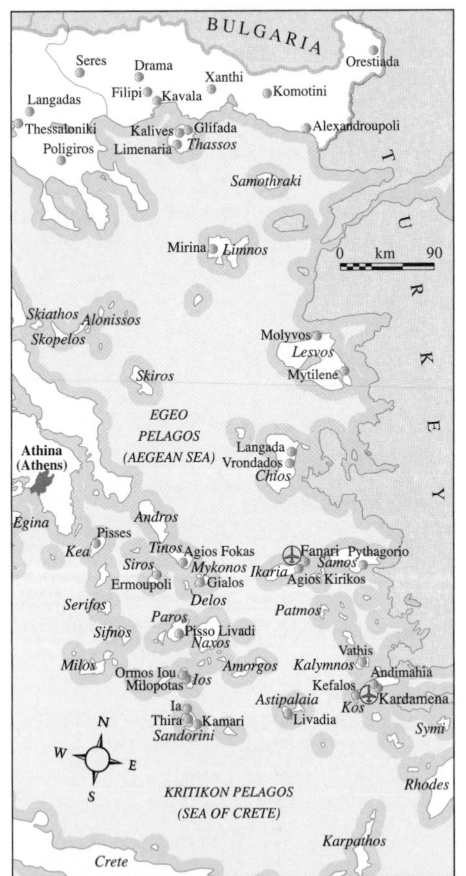
BULGARIA
Seres
Drama
Xanthi
Orestiada
Langadas
Filipi
Kavala
Komotini
Thessaloniki
Kalives
Glifada
Alexandroupoli
Poligiros
Limenaria
Thassos
Samothraki
TURKEY
Mirina
Limnos
0 km 90
Skiathos
Alonissos
Skopelos
Molyvos
Lesvos
Mytilene
Skiros
EGEO
PELAGOS
(AEGEAN SEA)
Langada
Vrondados
Chios
Athina
(Athens)
Egina
Andros
Pisses
Kea
Tinos
Agios Fokas
Fanari
Pythagorio
Siros
Mykonos
Ikaria
Samos
Ermoupoli
Gialos
Agios Kirikos
Serifos
Delos
Patmos
Paros
Sifnos
Pisso Livadi
Naxos
Vathis
Milos
Ormos Iou
Amorgos
Kalymnos
Andimahia
Milopotas
Ios
Kefalos
Astipalaia
Kardamena
Ia
Kos
Thira
Kamari
Livadia
Symi
Sandorini
N
W
E
S
KRITIKON PELAGOS
(SEA OF CRETE)
Rhodes
Karpathos
Crete

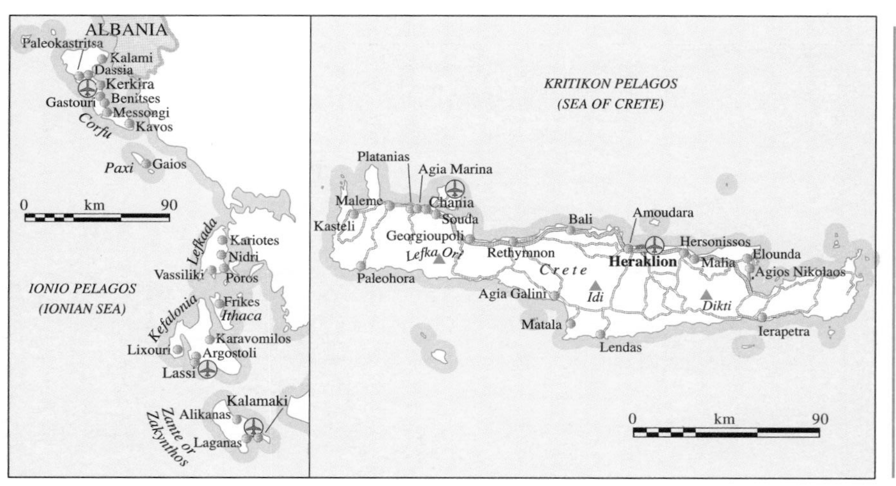
ALBANIA
Paleokastritsa
Kalami
Dassia
Kerkira
Gastouri
Benitses
Messongi
Kavos
Corfu
Paxi
Gaios
0
km
90
Lefkada
Kariotes
Nidri
Vassiliki
Poros
IONIO PELAGOS
(IONIAN SEA)
Frikes
Ithaca
Kefalonia
Karavomilos
Lixouri
Argostoli
Lassi
Kalamaki
Alikanas
Zante or
Zakynthos
Laganas
KRITIKON PELAGOS
(SEA OF CRETE)
Platanias
Agia Marina
Maleme
Chania
Souda
Kasteli
Georgioupoli
Lefka Ori
Paleohora
Rethymnon
Bali
Amoudara
Hersonissos
Elounda
Heraklion
Malia
Agios Nikolaos
Crete
Agia Galini
Idi
Dikti
Matala
Lendas
Ierapetra
0
km
90

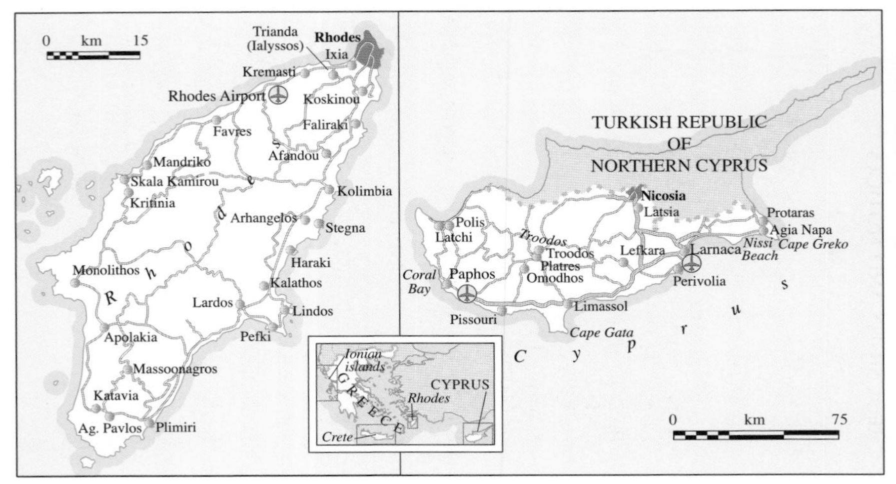
0 km 15
Trianda (Ialyssos)
Rhodes
Ixia
Kremasti
Rhodes Airport
Koskinou
Faliraki
Favres
Afandou
Mandriko
Skala Kamirou
Kritinia
Kolimbia
Arhangelos
Stegna
Haraki
Monolithos
Kalathos
Lardos
Lindos
Apolakia
Pefki
Massoonagros
Katavia
Ag. Pavlos
Plimiri
R h o d e s
TURKISH REPUBLIC OF NORTHERN CYPRUS
Nicosia
Latsia
Protaras
Polis
Latchi
Agia Napa
Troodos
Troodos
Platres
Omodhos
Lefkara
Larnaca
Nissi Beach
Cape Greko
Coral Bay
Paphos
Perivolia
Limassol
Pissouri
Cape Gata
C y p r u s
Ionian islands
GREECE
CYPRUS
Rhodes
Crete
0 km 75

GREEK SIGNS AND NOTICES

ΑΙΘΟΥΣΑ ΑΝΑΜΟΝΗΣ	*waiting room*
ΑΝΑΧΩΡΗΣΕΙΣ	*departures*
ΑΝΔΡΩΝ	*gents*
ΑΝΟΙΚΤΟΝ	*open*
ΑΠΑΓΟΡΕΥΕΤΑΙ Η ΕΙΣΟΔΟΣ	*no entry*
ΑΠΑΓΟΡΕΥΕΤΑΙ Η ΚΟΛΥΜΒΗΣΗ	*no swimming*
ΑΠΑΓΟΡΕΥΟΝΤΑΙ ΟΙ ΚΑΤΑΔΥΣΕΙΣ	*no diving*
ΑΠΑΓΟΡΕΥΕΤΑΙ ΤΟ ΚΑΠΝΙΣΜΑ	*no smoking*
ΑΠΑΓΟΡΕΥΕΤΑΙ Η ΣΤΑΘΜΕΥΣΗ	*no parking*
ΑΠΑΓΟΡΕΥΕΤΑΙ Ο ΓΥΜΝΙΣΜΟΣ	*nudism prohibited*
ΑΠΑΓΟΡΕΥΕΤΑΙ Η ΛΗΨΗ ΦΩΤΟΓΡΑΦΙΩΝ	*no photographs*
ΑΠΑΓΟΡΕΥΕΤΑΙ ΤΟ ΨΑΡΕΜΑ	*no fishing*
ΑΠΑΓΟΡΕΥΜΕΝΗ ΠΕΡΙΟΧΗ	*restricted area*
ΑΠΩΛΕΣΘΕΝΤΑ	*lost property*
ΑΣΤΥΝΟΜΙΑ	*police*
ΑΦΙΞΕΙΣ	*arrivals*
ΒΓΑΛΤΕ ΤΗΝ ΚΑΡΤΑ	*remove the phonecard*
ΓΙΑ ΕΞΩΤΕΡΙΚΗ ΧΡΗΣΗ ΜΟΝΟ	*for external use only*
ΓΙΑ ΕΣΩΤΕΡΙΚΗ ΧΡΗΣΗ ΜΟΝΟ	*for internal use only*

ΓΥΝΑΙΚΩΝ	*ladies*
ΔΕΝ ΛΕΙΤΟΥΡΓΕΙ	*out of order*
ΔΙΑΝΥΚΤΕΡΕΥΟΝ	*open all night*
ΔΙΟΔΙΑ	*toll*
ΕΘΝΙΚΗ ΟΔΟΣ	*motorway*
ΕΙΣΙΤΗΡΙΑ	*tickets*
ΕΙΣΟΔΟΣ	*entrance*
ΕΚΠΤΩΣΕΙΣ	*sales*
ΕΛΕΓΧΟΣ ΑΠΟΣΚΕΥΩΝ	*baggage control*
ΕΛΕΓΧΟΣ ΔΙΑΒΑΤΗΡΙΩΝ	*passport control*
ΕΛΕΥΘΕΡΟΝ	*vacant*
ΕΝΟΙΚΙΑΖΟΝΤΑΙ ΑΥΤΟΚΙΝΗΤΑ	*car rental*
ΕΝΟΙΚΙΑΖΟΝΤΑΙ ΔΩΜΑΤΙΑ	*rooms to let*
ΕΞΟΔΟΣ	*exit*
ΕΞΟΔΟΣ ΚΙΝΔΥΝΟΥ	*emergency exit*
ΕΞΩΤΕΡΙΚΟΥ	*overseas mail*
ΕΠΙΛΕΞΑΤΕ ΤΟΝ ΑΡΙΘΜΟ	*dial the number*
ΕΠΙΣΤΡΕΦΩ ΣΕ ΛΙΓΟ	*back in a little while*
ΕΡΓΑ	*roadworks*
ΕΣΩΤΕΡΙΚΟΥ	*inland mail*
ΖΕΣΤΟ	*hot*
ΗΜΕΡΟΜΗΝΙΑ ΛΗΞΕΩΣ	*best before*
ΙΔΙΩΤΙΚΟΣ ΔΡΟΜΟΣ	*private road*
ΚΑΤΕΙΛΗΜΜΕΝΟ	*engaged*
ΚΑΤΟΛΙΣΘΗΣΕΙΣ	*falling rocks*
ΚΙΝΔΥΝΟΣ	*danger*

ΚΛΕΙΣΤΟΝ	*closed*
ΚΡΥΟ	*cold*
Κ.Τ.Ε.Λ.	*long-distance bus station*
ΜΗ ΒΓΑΖΕΤΕ ΤΗΝ ΚΑΡΤΑ	*do not remove the phonecard yet*
ΜΗΝ ΑΓΓΙΖΕΤΕ	*do not touch*
ΜΗΝ ΕΝΟΧΛΕΙΤΕ	*do not disturb*
ΜΗ ΠΟΣΙΜΟ	*not for drinking*
ΝΟΣΟΚΟΜΕΙΟ	*hospital*
Ο.Σ.Ε.	*Greek Railways*
Ο.Τ.Ε.	*Greek Telecom*
ΠΛΗΡΕΣ	*no vacancies*
ΠΛΗΡΟΦΟΡΙΕΣ	*information*
ΠΟΣΙΜΟ ΝΕΡΟ	*drinking water*
ΠΡΟΣΟΧΗ	*caution*
ΠΡΟΣΟΧΗ ΕΞΟΔΟΣ ΟΧΗΜΑΤΩΝ	*caution: vehicle exit*
ΠΡΟΣΟΧΗ ΣΚΥΛΟΣ	*beware of the dog*
ΠΩΛΕΙΤΑΙ	*for sale*
ΡΕΣΕΨΙΟΝ	*reception*
ΣΥΡΑΤΕ	*pull*
ΤΑΜΕΙΟ	*cash desk*
ΤΕΛΩΝΕΙΟ	*customs*
ΤΟΥΑΛΕΤΕΣ	*toilets*
ΤΡΟΧΑΙΑ	*traffic police*
ΩΘΗΣΑΤΕ	*push*
ΩΡΕΣ ΛΕΙΤΟΥΡΓΙΑΣ	*opening hours*

Numbers

0	mithen	[μηδέν]
1	ena	[ένα]
2	thio	[δύο]
3	tria	[τρία]
4	tesera	[τέσσερα]
5	pendeh	[πέντε]
6	eksi	[έξι]
7	efta	[εφτά]
8	oKHto	[οχτώ]
9	enia	[εννιά]
10	theka	[δέκα]
11	endeka	[έντεκα]
12	thotheka	[δώδεκα]
13	thekatria	[δεκατρία]
14	thekatesera	[δεκατέσσερα]
15	thekapendeh	[δεκαπέντε]
16	theka-eksi	[δεκαέξι]
17	theka-efta	[δεκαεφτά]
18	theka-oKHto	[δεκαοχτώ]
19	theka-enia	[δεκαεννιά]
20	ikosi	[είκοσι]
21	ikosi ena	[είκοσι ένα]
22	ikosi thio	[είκοσι δύο]
23	ikosi tria	[είκοσι τρία]
24	ikosi tesera	[είκοσι τέσσερα]
25	ikosi pendeh	[είκοσι πέντε]
26	ikosi eksi	[είκοσι έξι]
27	ikosi efta	[είκοσι εφτά]
28	ikosi oKHto	[είκοσι οχτώ]
29	ikosi enia	[είκοσι εννιά]
30	trianda	[τριάντα]
31	trianda ena	[τριάντα ένα]
40	saranda	[σαράντα]
50	peninda	[πενήντα]
60	eksinda	[εξήντα]

70	evthominda	[εβδομήντα]
80	ogthonda	[ογδόντα]
90	eneninda	[ενενήντα]
100	ekato	[εκατό]
101	ekaton ena	[εκατόν ένα]
165	ekaton eksinda pendeh	[εκατόν εξήντα πέντε]
200	thiakosia	[διακόσια]
300	triakosia	[τριακόσια]
1,000	KHilia	[χίλια]
2,000	thio KHiliathes	[δύο χιλιάδες]
3,000	tris KHiliathes	[τρεις χιλιάδες]
4,655	teseris KHiliathes eksakosia peninda pendeh	[τέσσερις χιλιάδες εξακόσια πενήντα πέντε]
1,000,000	ena ekatomirio	[ένα εκατομμύριο]

NB: in Greek the comma is a decimal point; for thousands use a full stop, eg 6.000

Dates: *to say the date in Greek just use the ordinary number, eg:*

on the second of... stis thio...

Exceptions are:

on the 1st of... stis mia...
on the 3rd of... stis trees...
on the 4th of... stis teserees...
on the 13th of... stis thekatris...
on the 14th of... stis thekateseris...
on the 21st of... stis ikosi mia...
on the 23rd of... stis ikosi tris...
on the 24th of... stis ikosi teseris...
on the 31st of... stis trianda mia...

The Greek Alphabet

Α	α	άλφα	ALFA	a *as in Anne*
Β	β	βήτα	VITA	v
Γ	γ	γάμμα	GAMA	g *as in go or* y *as in yes*
Δ	δ	δέλτα	THELTA	th *as in that*
Ε	ε	έψιλον	EPSILON	e *as in end*
Ζ	ζ	ζήτα	ZITA	z *as in zero*
Η	η	ήτα	ITA	i *as in pin*
Θ	θ	θήτα	THITA	TH *as in theatre*
Ι	ι	γιώτα	YOTA	i *as in pin*
Κ	κ	κάπα	KAPA	k
Λ	λ	λάμδα	LAMTHA	l
Μ	μ	μι	MI	m
Ν	ν	νι	NI	n
Ξ	ξ	ξι	KSI	x
Ο	ο	όμικρον	OMIKRON	o *as in hot*
Π	π	πι	PI	p
Ρ	ρ	ρο	RO	r
Σ	σ,ς*	σίγμα	SIGMA	s
Τ	τ	ταυ	TAF	t
Υ	υ	ύψιλον	IPSILON	i *as in pin*
Φ	φ	φι	FI	f
Χ	χ	χι	KHI	KH *as in Scottish loch*
Ψ	ψ	ψι	PSI	ps
Ω	ω	ωμέγα	OMEGA	o *as in hot*

* used only at the end of a word